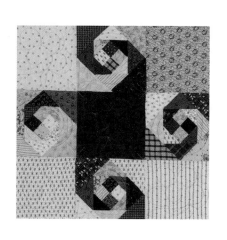

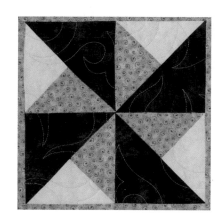

Published by: Kansas City Star Books
1729 Grand Blvd.
Kansas City, Missouri, USA 64108

First edition, first printing
ISBN: 978-1-935362-29-6

Library of Congress Control Number:
2009924512

Printed in the United States of America by Walsworth Publishing Co., Marceline, Missouri

To order copies, call toll-free 866-834-7467.

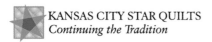

KANSAS CITY STAR QUILTS
Continuing the Tradition

The Quilter's Home Page

www.PickleDish.com
www.PickleDishStore.com

My Stars II

Patterns from The Kansas City Star • Volume II

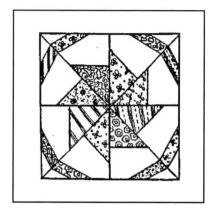
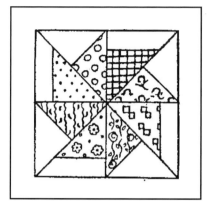
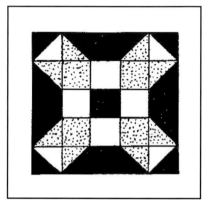
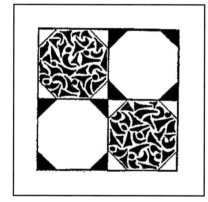

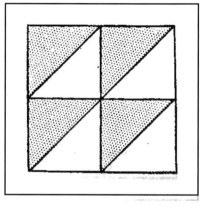
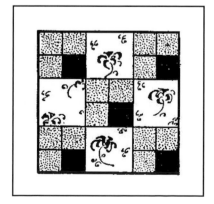
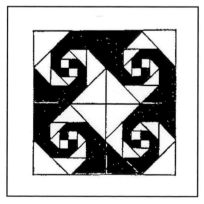
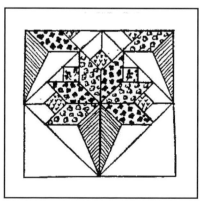

In April 2009, Kansas City Star Quilts published *My Stars: Patterns from The Kansas City Star, Volume I* to much success. We decided to make this a series, so eventually all of the historical Kansas City Star patterns will be redrafted and published by the same company that printed them decades ago.

In *Volume I*, we asked you, our readers and quilters, to submit their quilts that matched the patterns offered in the book. We loved receiving all of the photos and getting to see the beautiful work that you have accomplished. The photos that were chosen – we wish we could have included them all – really enhanced the project. So we decided to repeat the process for *Volume II*.

We received even more submissions this second time around, and wow, what a great selection of quilts. We had so much trouble choosing! Because of that, we have increased the number of photos in the book – seven of the 25 patterns will include a photograph of a quilt by a fellow quilter friend.

My Stars II includes 25 more patterns that were offered to My Star Collection subscribers, a program that provides a web download of a redrafted pattern each week. Each pattern in the book includes fabric requirements, templates and assembly instructions, as well as the original caption that was printed in the newspaper.

So whether you plan to stitch these famous old blocks or are a collector, sit back and enjoy the heritage of quilting. And clear a spot on your shelf, because eventually Kansas City Star Quilts will chronicle them all. This is only the second of many more to come.

Diane McLendon
Editor

* * *

Kansas City Star Quilts would like to thank the wonderful team that has made My Star Collection and the *My Stars* series possible: Edie McGinnis, Jenifer Dick, Kim Walsh, Doug Weaver, Aaron Leimkuehler, Jo Ann Groves, and of course, our quilt friends who have graciously provided their quilts to be included in this book.

Diane McLendon
Editor

* * *

My Star Collection is a weekly subscription service where subscribers download a pdf pattern – from The Kansas City Star's historical 1928 to 1961 collection – each week. The subscription is for a year of patterns – 52 in all. For more information or to sign up, visit subscriptions.pickledish.com.

TABLE OF CONTENTS

May Basket

Block Size: 6" finished

Fabric Needed:

Off-White

Medium blue

Dark blue

Cutting Directions

From the off-white, cut

1 - 4 7/8" square. Cut the square once from corner to corner on the diagonal to make 2 triangles or cut 2 triangles using template A.

2 - 2 1/2" squares (template B)

From the medium blue, cut

1 - 4 7/8" square. Cut the square once from corner to corner on the diagonal to make 2 triangles or cut 1 triangle using template A. (If you cut the square, you will have one triangle left over.)

From the dark blue, cut

1 - 2 7/8" square. Cut the square once from corner to corner on the diagonal to make 2 triangles or cut 2 triangles using template C.

1 basket handle using template D

To Make the Block

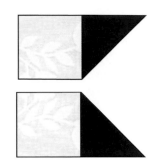

1 Sew a dark blue C triangle to the off-white B square.

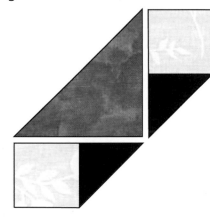

2 Sew the B-C units to the medium blue triangle.

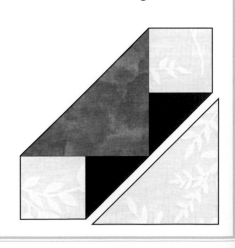

3 Now add an off-white A triangle.

4 Appliqué the basket handle to the remaining off-white A triangle.

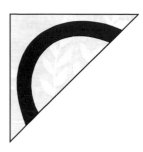

5 Sew the handle unit to the top of the basket.

6 Make four baskets if you would like your block to measure 12-inches. If the handles of all four are turned towards the center, your block will look like the stamps issued by the post office 25 years ago.

From The Kansas City Star, July 2, 1941:

Number 651

This version of a May basket was originated by Mrs. Roy Bevis, Rock, Kas., and sent to The Weekly Star by Mrs. H. H. Bevis, Route 1, Sedan, Kas. The handle of the basket is appliqued on the large upper triangle. It is suggested that the basket be of print and the handle of a one-tone material of a color predominating in the print.

History of the Block

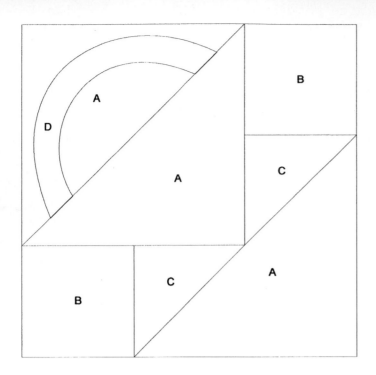

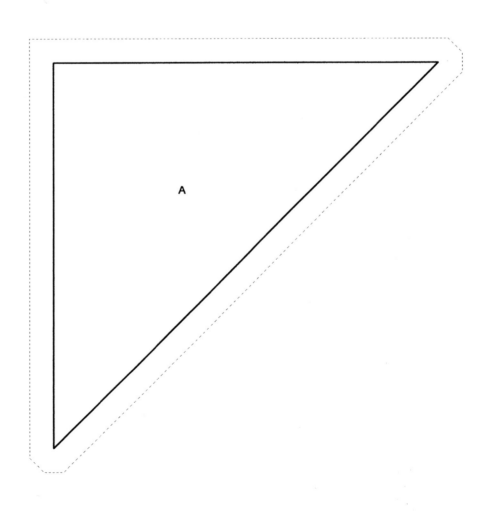

A

Template

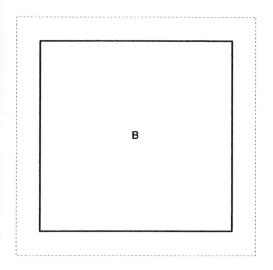

B

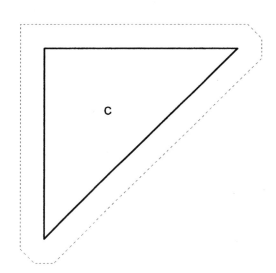

C

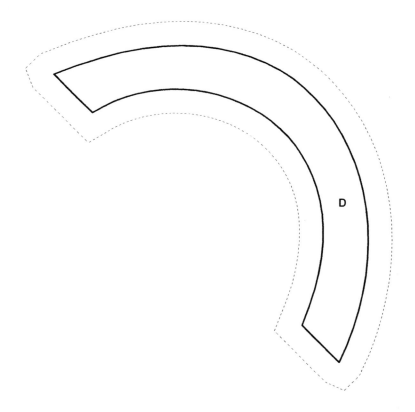

D

May Basket

Template

Flying Kite

Block Size: 12" finished

Appeared in The Star **July 7, 1937**

Fabric Needed:

Striped

Orange (or something that complements your choice of striped fabric)

Background

Cutting Directions

From the background fabric, cut

4 triangles using template A

4 strips using template B

From the striped fabric, cut

4 triangles using template C

From the orange fabric, cut

4 triangles using template A

To Make the Block

1 Sew a background A triangle to an orange A triangle. Make four of these units.

2 Sew a striped C triangle to a background B piece. Make four of these units

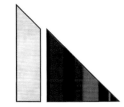

3 Sew the units together as shown to make one-fourth of the block.

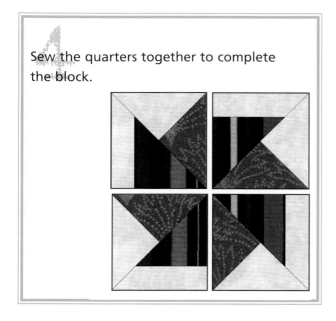

4 Sew the quarters together to complete the block.

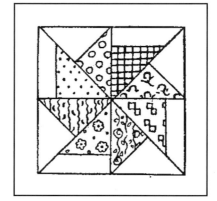

From The Kansas City Star,

July 7, 1937:

Number 509

This simple and effective quilt pattern was contributed to The Star by Mrs. Everett Royster, Silex, Mo. Thank you.

History of the Block

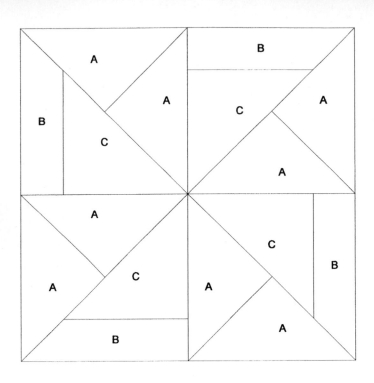

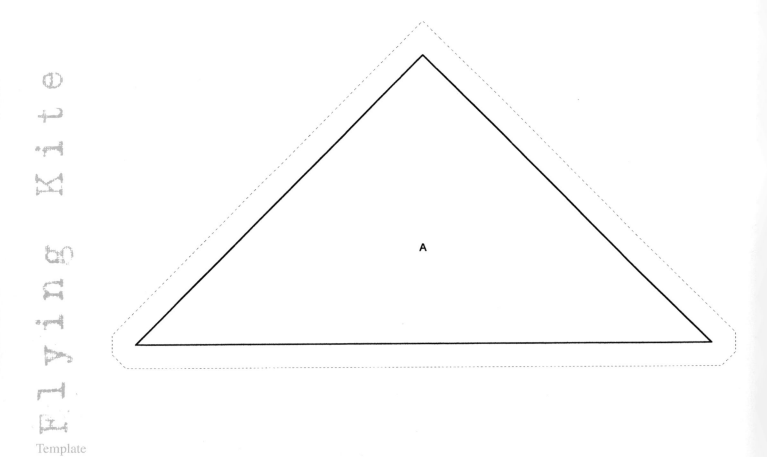

A

Template

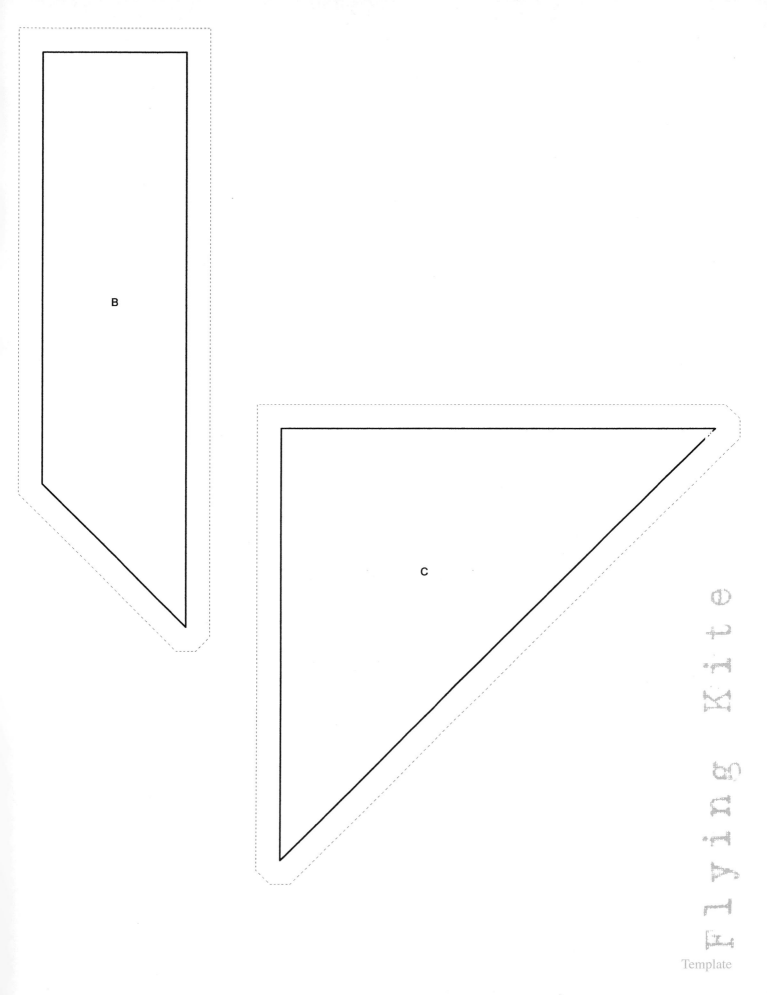

B

C

Flying Kite

Depression

Block Size: 12" finished

Appeared in The Star **March 20, 1937**

Fabric Needed:

Light blue

Medium blue

Blue print

Dark blue

Cutting Directions

From the dark blue fabric, cut

2 – 3 7/8" squares or 4 triangles using template A

From the blue print fabric, cut

6 – 3 7/8" squares or 12 triangles using template A

From the medium blue fabric, cut

6 – 3 7/8" squares or 12 triangles using template A

From the light blue fabric, cut

2 – 3 7/8" squares or 4 triangles using template A

To Make the Block

If you cut squares, draw a line from corner to corner on the diagonal on the reverse side of the lightest fabrics. Place 2 of the print squares atop the 2 dark squares with right sides facing and sew 1/4" on either side of the line. Using your rotary cutter, cut on the line. Open each of the half-square triangle units and press toward the dark fabric.

Place the 2 light squares atop 2 of the medium squares and make half-square triangles following the above directions.

Place the remaining print squares atop the remaining medium squares and make half-square triangles following the above directions.

If you cut triangles, sew them together to make the following half-square triangle units.
4 – dark/print
8 – medium/print
4 – light/medium

Depression

2

Sew the half-square triangle units into rows as shown.

1

Sew the rows together to complete the block .

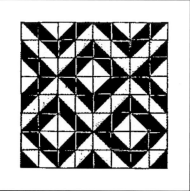

From The Kansas City Star,

March 20, 1937:

Number 495

An Oklahoma woman says she designed this quilt a year or so ago and named it "Depression" because she heard so many persons say they had difficulty making ends meet at that time. The pattern was contributed by Mrs. Charles C. Ross, Claremore, Ok.

History of the Block

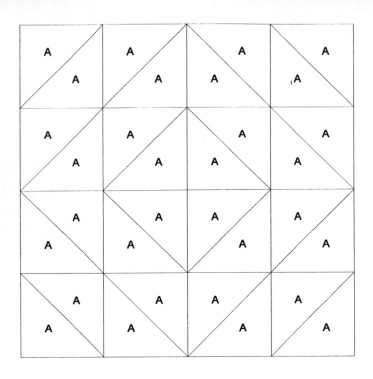

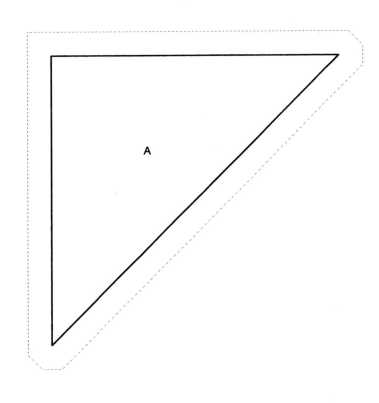

Template

Townsend Square designed and quilted by Linda Thielfoldt, Troy, Mich.

Puss in the Corner

Block Size: 12" finished

First appeared in The Star **November 5, 1932**

To Make the Block

1

Sew two brown A squares together and one brown and light green print square together. Sew the pairs together to make a four-patch unit. Make five units like this.

2

Sew the four-patch units and the squares together in rows as shown below to complete the block.

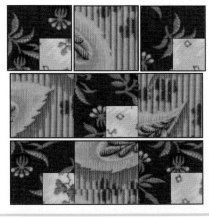

Fabric Needed:

Light green print

Brown and pink print

Pink and green print

Cutting Directions

From the light green print fabric, cut

5 - 2 1/2" squares (template A)

From the brown and pink print fabric, cut

15 - 2 1/2" squares (template A)

From the pink and green fabric, cut

4 – 4 1/2" squares (template B)

Puss in the Corner

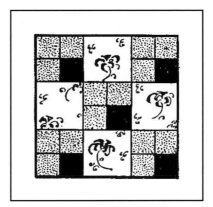

From The Kansas City Star,

November 5, 1932:

Number 270

What a cunning variation of the old-time 9-patch, and so easy to make, too. The charm of it lies in the unusual placing of the small dark squares. This makes a 12-inch block, but if a daintier effect is desired, cut down the size. Allow seams.

From The Kansas City Star,

June 17, 1933:

Number 310

Several requests have come for a quilt which a little girl may piece during vacation. We look over our files and select "Puss in the Corner" as an easy pattern which makes a pretty quilt. Allow for seams. All edges are straight. This is a repeated pattern.

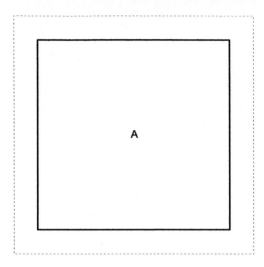

Template

Appeared in The Star **February 28, 1940**

Little Cedar Tree

Block Size: 12" finished

Fabric Needed:

Dark green

Medium green

Tan

To Make the Block

1 Sew a medium green triangle to a tan triangle, making a half-square triangle. Make two units like this.

2 Sew a tan triangle to a dark green triangle. You only need one unit like this.

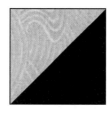

3 Now sew a medium green triangle to a dark green triangle, making a half-square triangle.

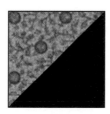

Cutting Directions

From the dark green fabric, cut

1 – 6 7/8" square. Cut the square once from corner to corner on the diagonal to make 2 triangles or cut 2 triangles using template A.

From the medium green fabric, cut

2 – 6 7/8" squares or 3 triangles using template A. If you cut the squares, cut them once from corner to corner on the diagonal.

From the tan fabric, cut

2 – 6 7/8" squares or 3 triangles using template A. If you cut the squares, cut them once from corner to corner on the diagonal.

Little Cedar Tree

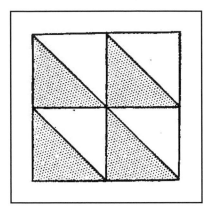

From The Kansas City Star,

February 28, 1940:

Number 608

Even the inexperienced quilt maker need not hesitate to undertake the task of making a quilt of this design. Green and white are unquestionably appropriate.

4 Sew the four units together as shown to complete the block.

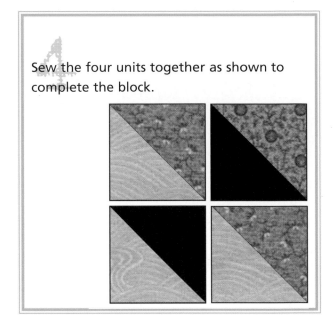

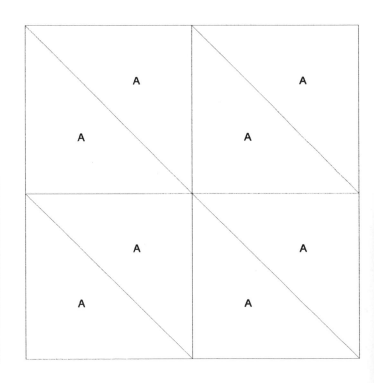

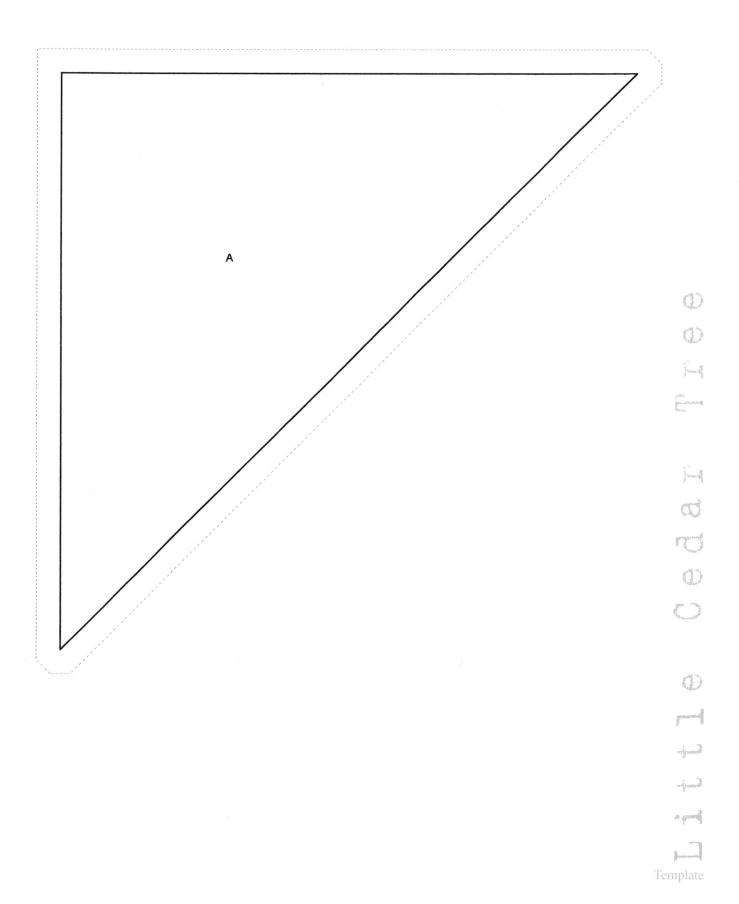

A

Template

The Red, the White, the Blue

Block Size: 12" finished

Fabric Needed:

Red and white print

Blue print

Red

Cutting Directions

From the red fabric, cut

8 pieces using template A

8 pieces using template C

From the red and white print fabric, cut

8 pieces using template A

8 pieces using template C

From the blue fabric, cut

16 pieces using template B

The Red, the White, the Blue

To Make the Block

1 Sew a red C piece to a blue B piece. Add a red A piece. You'll have a triangle that looks like this. Make 4.

2 Sew a red and white print C piece to a blue B piece. Then add a red and white print A piece. Make 4.

3 Sew a red C piece to a blue B piece and add a red and white print A piece. Make 4.

4 Sew a red and white print C piece to a blue B piece. Add a red A piece. Make 4.

5 Sew the triangles together to make squares as shown below. Make 2 of each.

Sew the four squares together to complete the block.

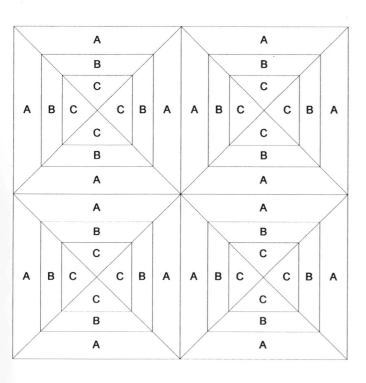

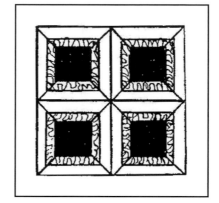

From The Kansas City Star,

December 14, 1955:

Number 969

Employing our national colors, the border of this design alternates small squares of red and white.

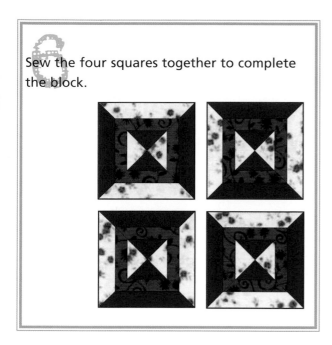

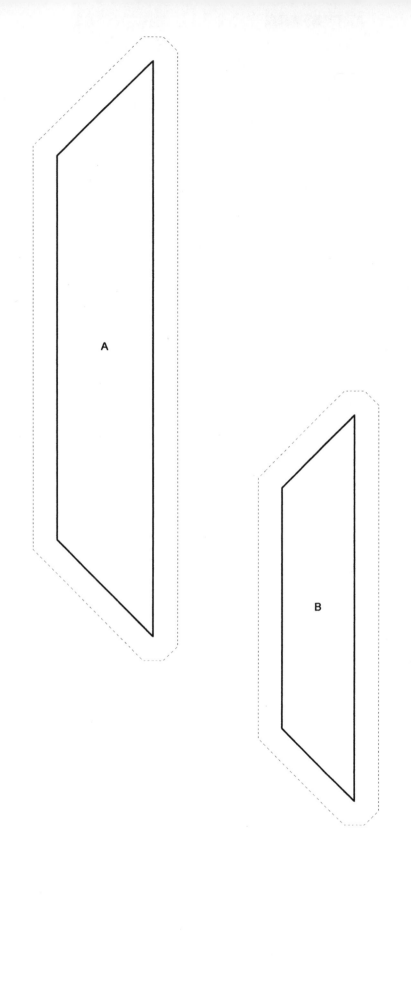

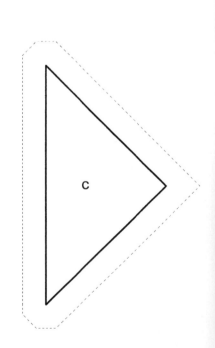

Template

Appeared in The Star **October 3, 1928**

To Make the Block

1 Sew the tan ovals (piece E) to the medium blue D pieces.

2 Sew the center of the block together.

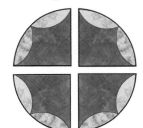

3 Sew a dark blue C triangle to either side of a tan B triangle. Make 4 of these units.

4 Sew the C-B-C units to the center of the block.

French Star

Block Size: 12" finished

Fabric Needed:

Tan

Medium blue

Dark blue

Cutting Directions

From the tan fabric, cut

4 squares using template A

4 triangles using template B

8 ovals using template E

From the medium blue, cut

4 pieces using template D

From the dark blue, cut

8 triangles using template C

French Star

From The Kansas City Star,

October 3, 1928:

Number 3

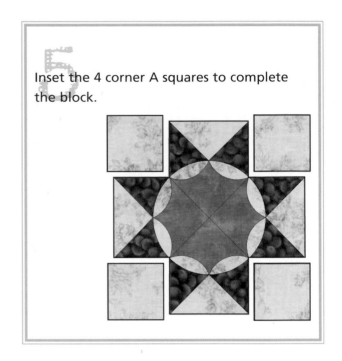

Inset the 4 corner A squares to complete the block.

No collection of quilt block designs is complete without one in a star motif. With the pioneer mothers who so ingeniously planned and pieced their own quilts, this symbol was a favorite. The French Star is a Canadian pattern varying the eight pointed star of diamond-shaped blocks by introducing small melon-shaped pieces of the background color or of contrasting hue. These melon-shaped pieces in turn form a wreath and may divide the star into two colors, as rose and pink, two shades of green or orange and yellow, as suggested. Make the patterns of cardboard of exactly the same size they are sketched above. Then lay the cardboard patterns on the cloth, and trace around with a pencil. These patterns do not allow for a seam, so when you cut them out of the cloth cut the cloth larger to make a seam of the width desired and then sew back to the pencil line. In making the French Star, sew two of the cone-shaped pieces to each white triangle, and then sew the corner squares to two of these blocks. The small melon-shaped blocks piece onto the center blocks; these in turn sew into a circle to which are added to oblong blocks and strips which were made first. This takes precise piecing, but it makes an usually attractive design when complete, either for patchwork pillows or for a quilt top. For the quilt, piece the star blocks together, using alternate squares of white of exactly the same size as the pieced blocks, and finish with a border of white or color as desired.

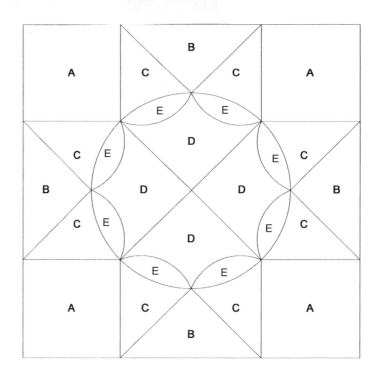

A

French Star

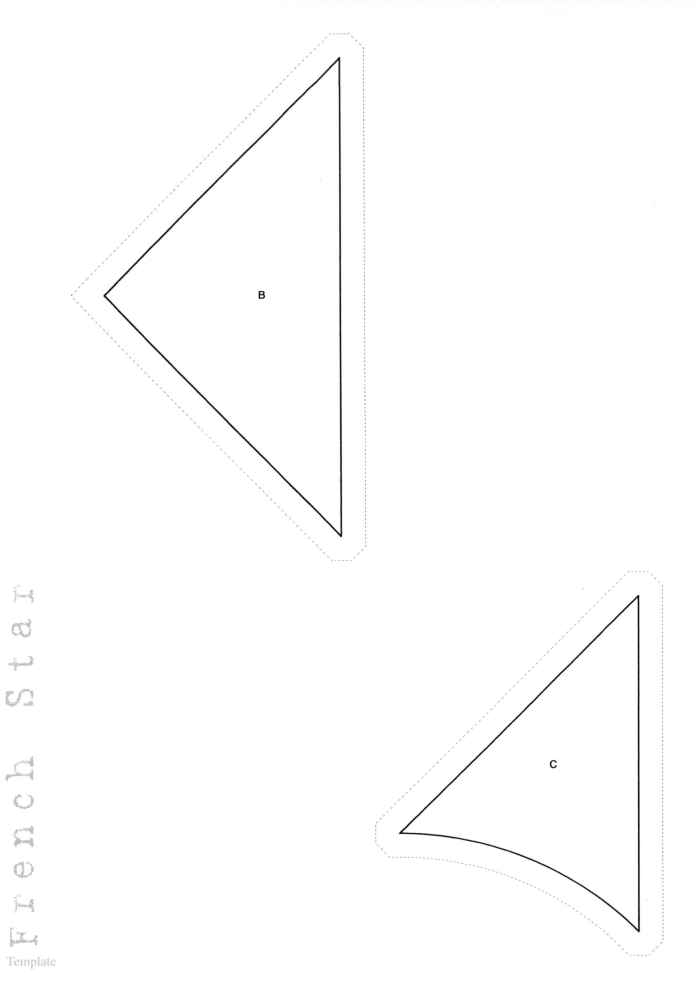

B

C

Template

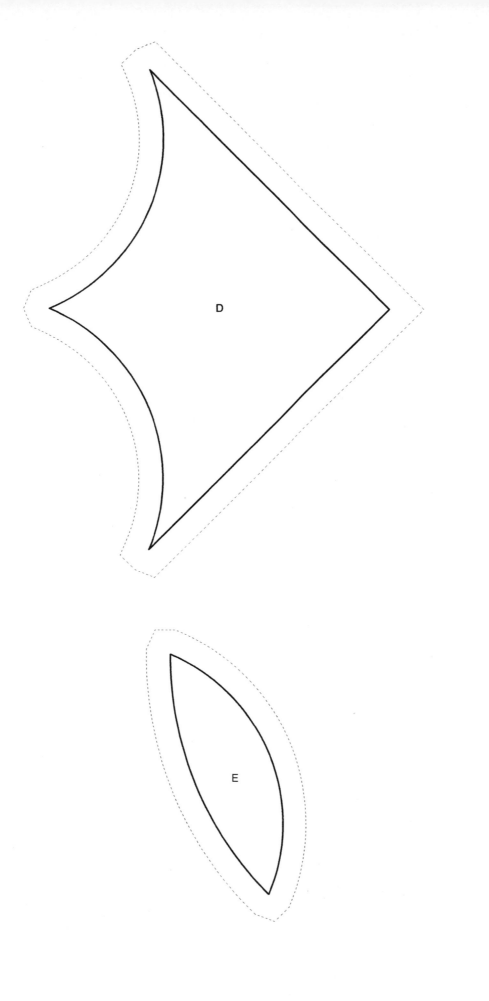

D

E

Template

Star of France designed and quilted by Martha Linville, Lee's Summit, Mo.

Calico Puzzle
Block Size: 12" finished

To Make the Block

If you cut squares, draw a line from corner to corner on the diagonal on the reverse side of the dark tan fabric. Place the tan squares atop the green squares with right sides facing and sew 1/4" on either side of the line. Using your rotary cutter, cut on the line. Open each of the half-square triangle units and press toward the dark fabric. You should have 16 half-square triangles.

If you chose to cut the triangles using template A, sew the tan and green triangles together to make 16 half-square triangles.

Sew the half-square triangle units and the squares together into rows as shown.

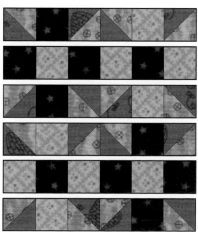

Fabric Needed:

Light tan

Dark tan

Brown print

Green

Cutting Directions

From the green fabric, cut

8 – 2 7/8" squares or 16 triangles

using template A

From the dark tan fabric, cut

8 – 2 7/8" squares or 16 triangles

using template A

From the light tan fabric, cut

10 – 2 1/2" squares or use template B

From the brown print fabric, cut

10 – 2 1/2" squares or use template B

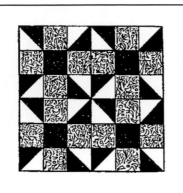

From The Kansas City Star,

September 13, 1930:

Number 114

The gay "Calico Puzzle" is really a very simple but effective combination of squares and triangles, in fact, a modernized variation of the historical "nine-patch." Any pretty color combination may be used, and while the block is only six inches square (four being shown above) it works up quickly and is a delight to the eye. Green for the solid color and yellow figured fabric with a small design combine nicely, and make a very pretty quilt. The quilt may be pieced in stripes if desired. No seams are allowed.

Sew the rows together to complete the block.

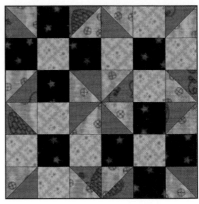

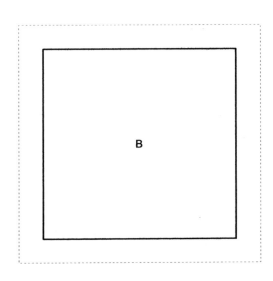

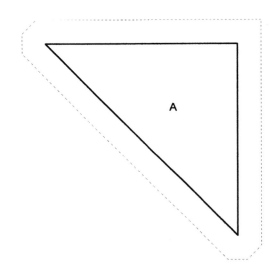

A

B

Calico Puzzle

Template

First appeared in The Star **August 26, 1933**

Jack in the Pulpit

Block Size: 12" finished

Fabric Needed:

Green print, Pink print, Light tan

Cutting Directions

From the light tan, cut

4 - 3 7/8" squares

(or cut 8 triangles using template A)

1 - 5 1/4" square. Cut the square twice from

corner to corner on the diagonal to make

4 triangles (or cut 4 triangles using template C)

From the pink, cut

1 - 4 1/2" square (Template B)

2 - 3 7/8" squares

(or cut 4 triangles using template A)

From the green, cut

2 - 3 7/8" squares

(or 4 triangles using template A)

4 rectangles using template D

(This template measures 7 9/16" x 1 15/16".)

To Make the Block

1

Begin at the top of the square and sew the first strip on leaving the seam open at the beginning. Start sewing about an inch away from the edge of the square.

2

Sew the green rectangles to the center square. Notice that the strips overlap. You'll need to leave the first strip open at the end of the seam rather than closing it as you would normally do.

Begin at the top of the square and sew the first strip on leaving the seam open at the end. Stop sewing about an inch away from the end of the square.

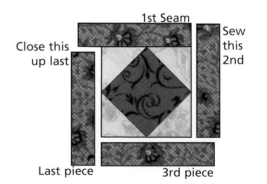

Sew the strips on, then go back and close up the first seam.

Now you need to make the corner units. First you need to make four half-square triangles. If you cut the pink and green A triangles, sew them together and press the seam toward the darkest fabric. If you cut squares, draw a line on the reverse side of the pink ones. Place a pink square atop a green square. Sew 1/4" on each side of the line. Use your rotary cutter and cut on the line. Open each unit and press toward the darkest fabric.

Sew a tan A triangle to the half-square triangles as shown. Make 4 of these corner units.

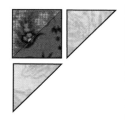

Sew the corner units to the center of the block.

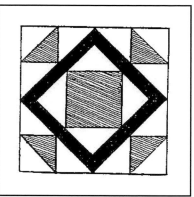

From The Kansas City Star, August 26, 1933:
Number 320

The straight line pattern of this "Jack-in-the-Pulpit" is easy to cut and easy to piece. Allow for seams.

From The Kansas City Star, March 22, 1944:
Number 740

This is the conception of J. D. Rhodes, route 1, Lake Village, Ark., of Jack-in-the-pulpit. The design was copied from a quilt made by his grandmother.

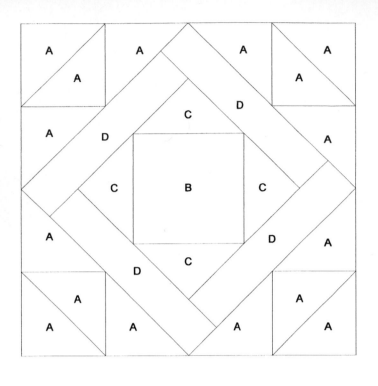

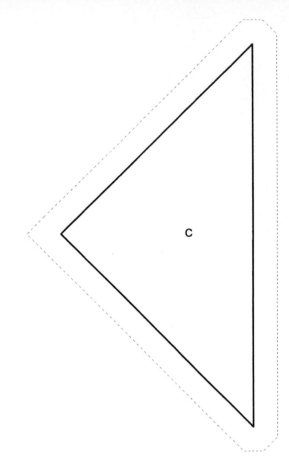

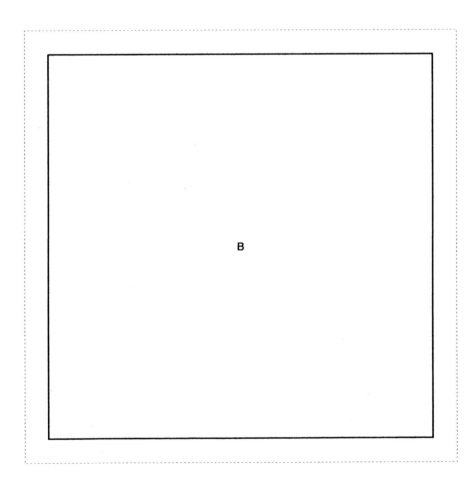

Jack in the Pulpit

Template

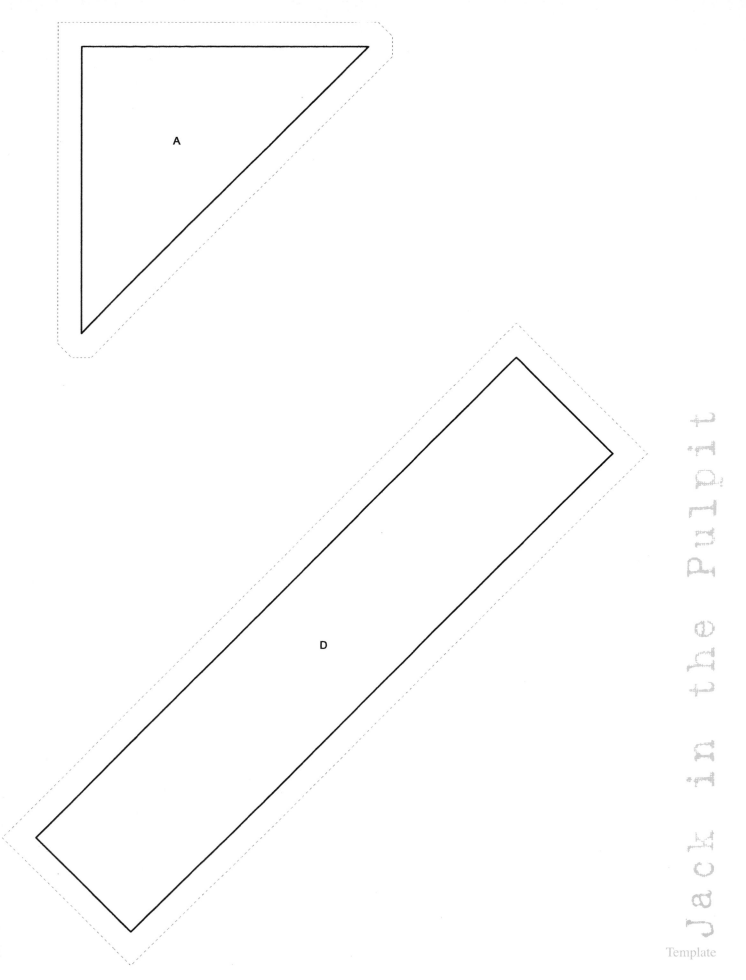

A

D

Jack in the Pulpit

Template

Nosegays

Block Size: 12" finished

Fabric Needed:
Green
Six assorted prints
Red
Off-white background

Cutting Directions
From the background fabric, cut
3 rectangles using template A
3 rectangles using template D
2 triangles using template B
1 piece using template G
1 piece using template C
1 piece using template F
1 pieces using template E

From the green fabric, cut
3 pieces using template K
2 pieces using template L

From the red fabric, cut
1 pieces using template M
1 piece using template H

From the assorted prints, cut
3 diamonds using template I
3 diamonds using template K

To Make the Block

1 Three of the leaf units are made by sewing piece D to piece K then adding piece A.

2 The remaining two leaf units are made by sewing a green L piece to a background C piece and a background G piece. Complete the units by adding triangle B.

3 Sew the I and J diamonds together into pairs.

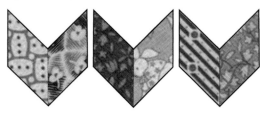

4 Sew the red M and H triangles together.

Nosegays

5 Add the background F and E pieces.

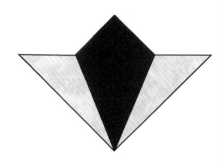

6 Stitch the diamond pairs on next as shown.

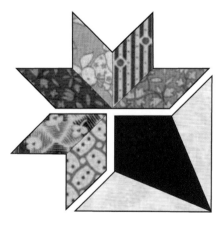

7 Inset the A-D-K , B-G-L and B-C-L leaf units in place as shown to complete the block.

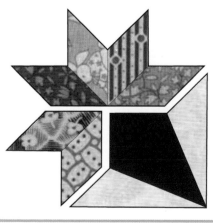

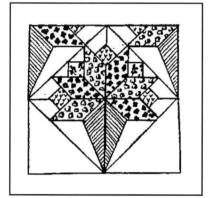

From The Kansas City Star, February 6, 1937:

Number 489

This is an excellent design to try when you desire to make use of odds and ends in your scrap bag. All diamonds and squares may be made of prints. The pattern was contributed by Mrs. Anna A. Threlkeld, Waynesville, Mo.

History of the Block

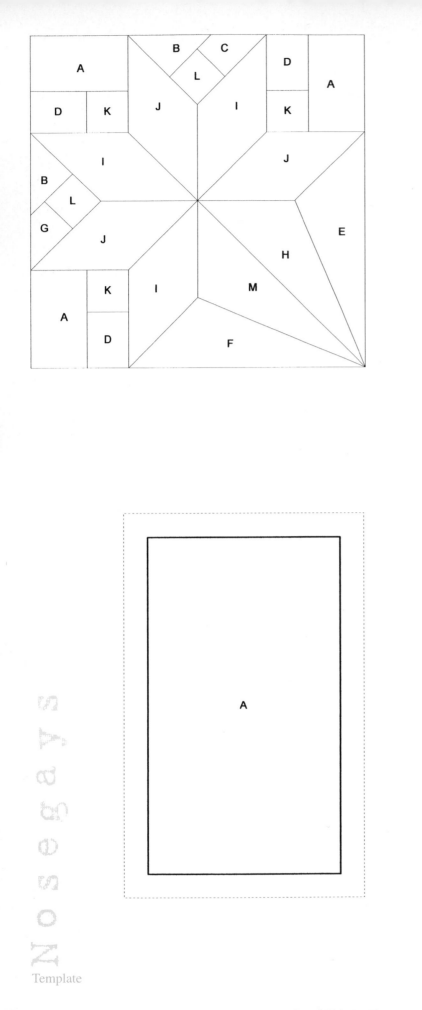

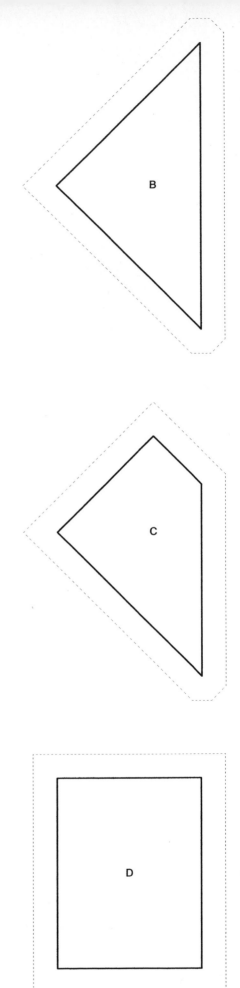

Nosegays

Template

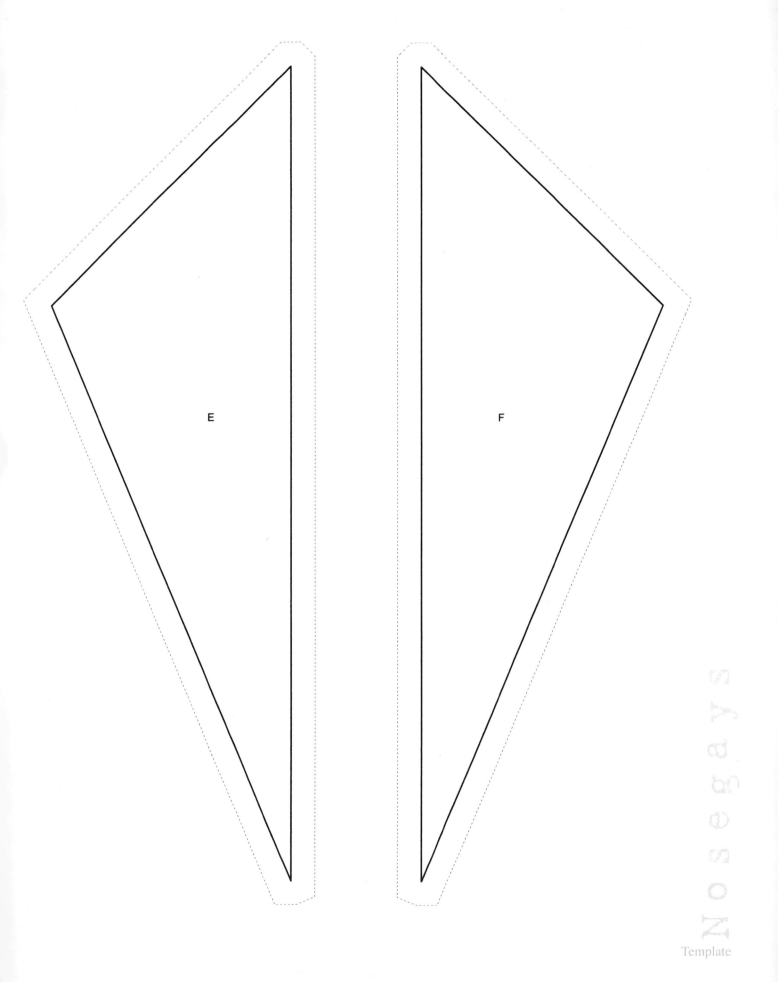

E

F

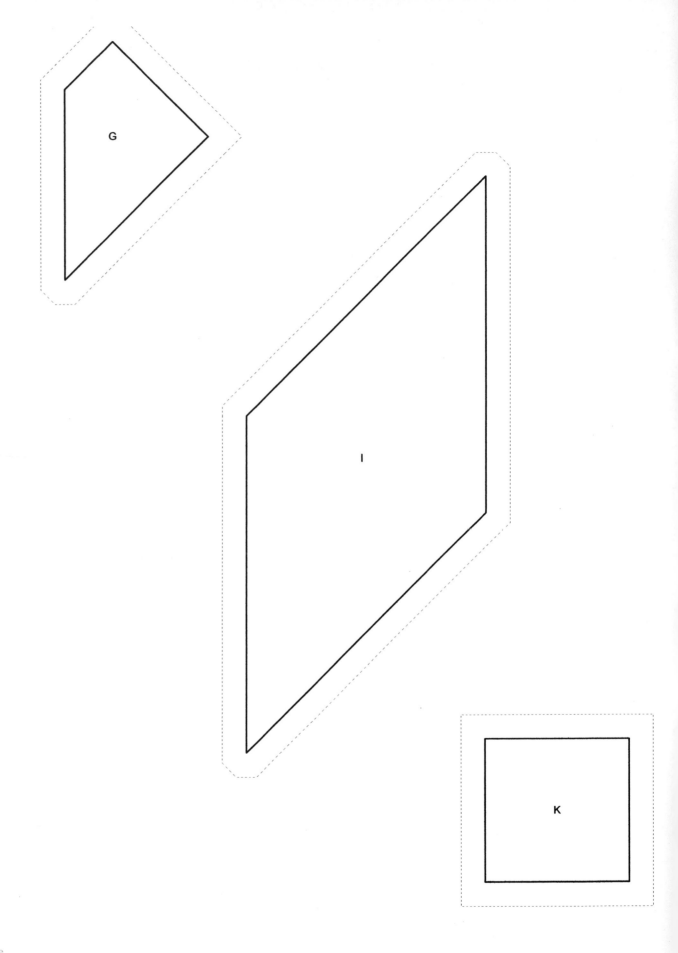

G

I

K

Nosegays

Template

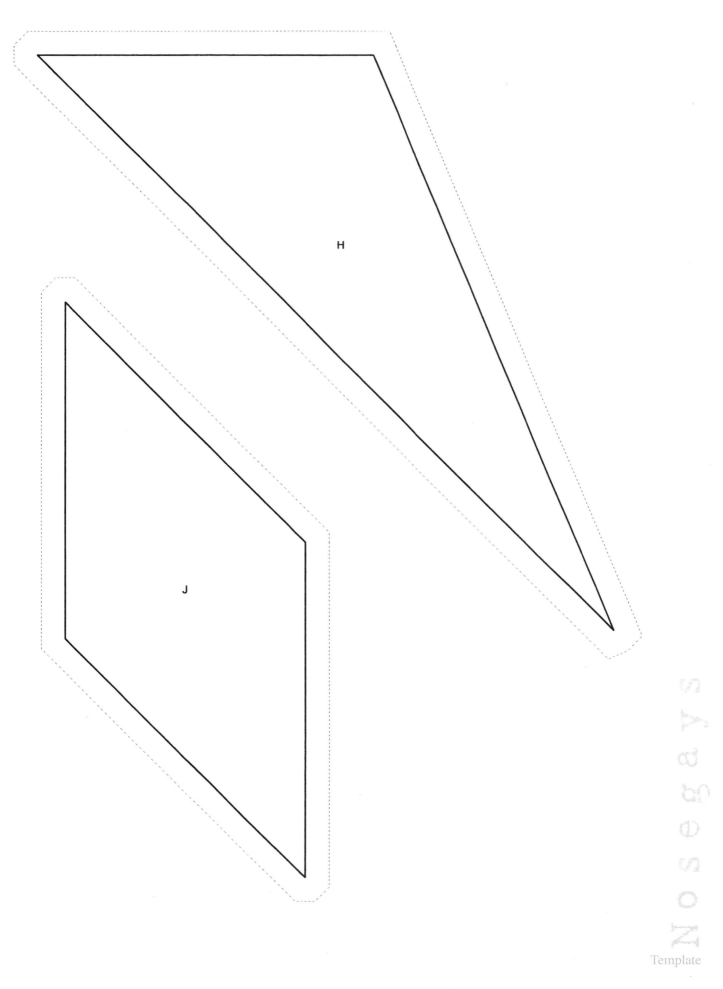

H

J

Nosegays

Template

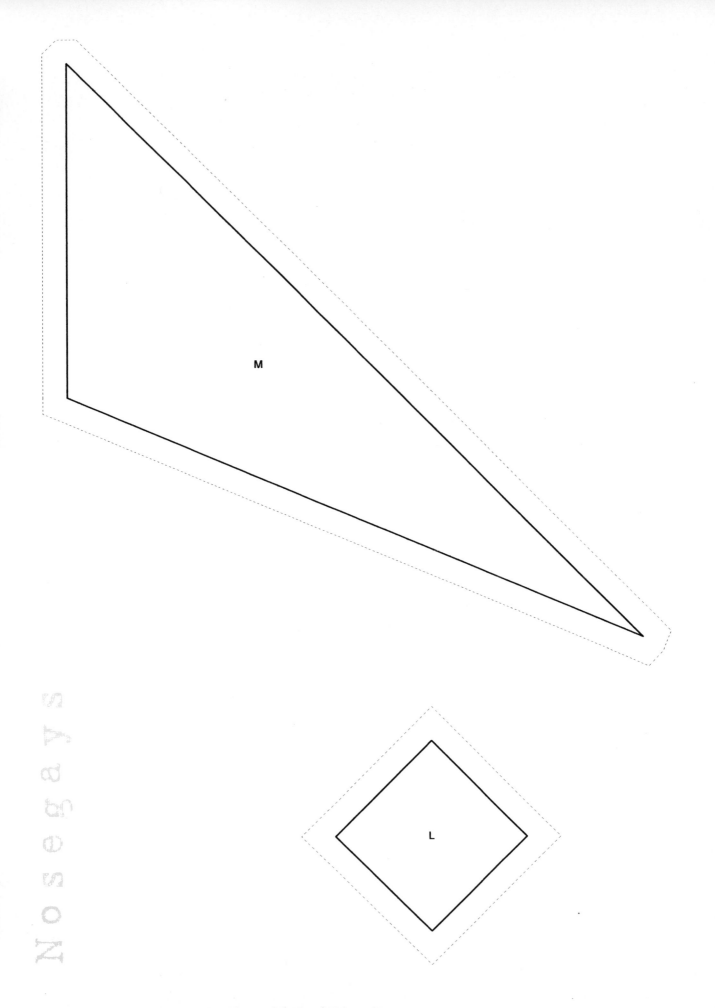

M

L

Nosegays

Nosegay owned by Susan Martin, Olathe, KS. Original quilter unknown.

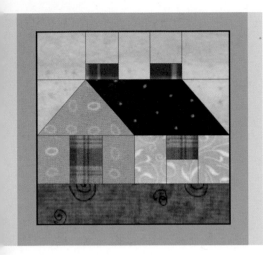

House on the Hill

Block Size: 12" finished

Fabric Needed:
Blue
Light tan
Medium tan
Dark brown
Red plaid
Tan and red plaid
Green

Cutting Directions
From the blue fabric, cut
2 – 3 1/2" squares (template A)
2 – 2 1/2" squares (template B)
1 – 3 1/2" x 2 1/2" rectangle (template C)
1 triangle using template D
1 triangle using template F

From the red plaid, cut
2 – 2 1/2" x 1 1/2" rectangles (template I)

From the green, cut
1 – 12 1/2" x 3" rectangle
(This is piece E and no template is given.)

From the medium tan, cut
1 triangle using template J
2 – 3 1/2" x 2 1/2" rectangles (template C)

From the light tan, cut
2 – 3 1/2" x 2 1/2" rectangles (template C)
1 – 2 1/2" x 2" rectangle (template G)

From the red and tan plaid, cut
1 – 3 1/2" x 2 1/2" rectangle (template C)
1 – 2 1/2" x 2" rectangle (template G)

From the dark brown, cut
3 pieces using template H

House on the Hill

To Make the Block

1 Sew the red plaid I rectangles to the blue B rectangles. Sew the pieces for the top strip together as shown.

2 Sew the three dark brown H pieces together. Add the medium tan J triangle to the left. Now sew a blue triangle to both ends to complete this strip.

3 Next sew the medium tan C strips to either side of the red and tan plaid C strip.

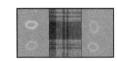

4 Sew the red and tan plaid G rectangle to the light tan G rectangle. Add a light tan C rectangle to either side as shown. Sew the two pieces together to complete this row.

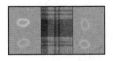

5 Sew the rows together as shown to complete the block.

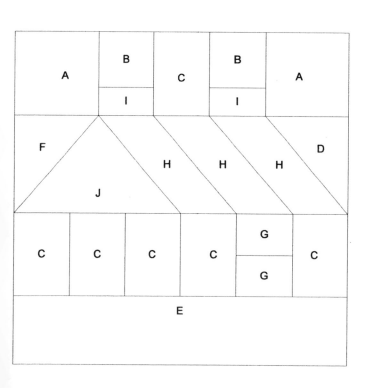

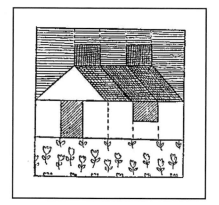

From The Kansas City Star, May 11, 1929:
Number 34

Now that The Star and its readers are thinking about The Star's exhibition homes, it is appropriate that we should present a little house quilt block pattern. The design was contributed by one of our readers. In a quilt it resembles houses on a street. It may be made of such colors as you have always imagined in your dream home, be it red-roofed or green. The "green lawn" in the foreground may be plain light green or sprigged. It should be 3-1/2 inches by 12-1/2 inches. One block makes an attractive cushion. All is cut a seam larger than the patterns mark. The finished blocks should be set together with green or print lattice strips about five or six inches wide to place the houses apart on the quilt. Quite a wide border of ivory, blue, coral and green strips would make a lovely edge.

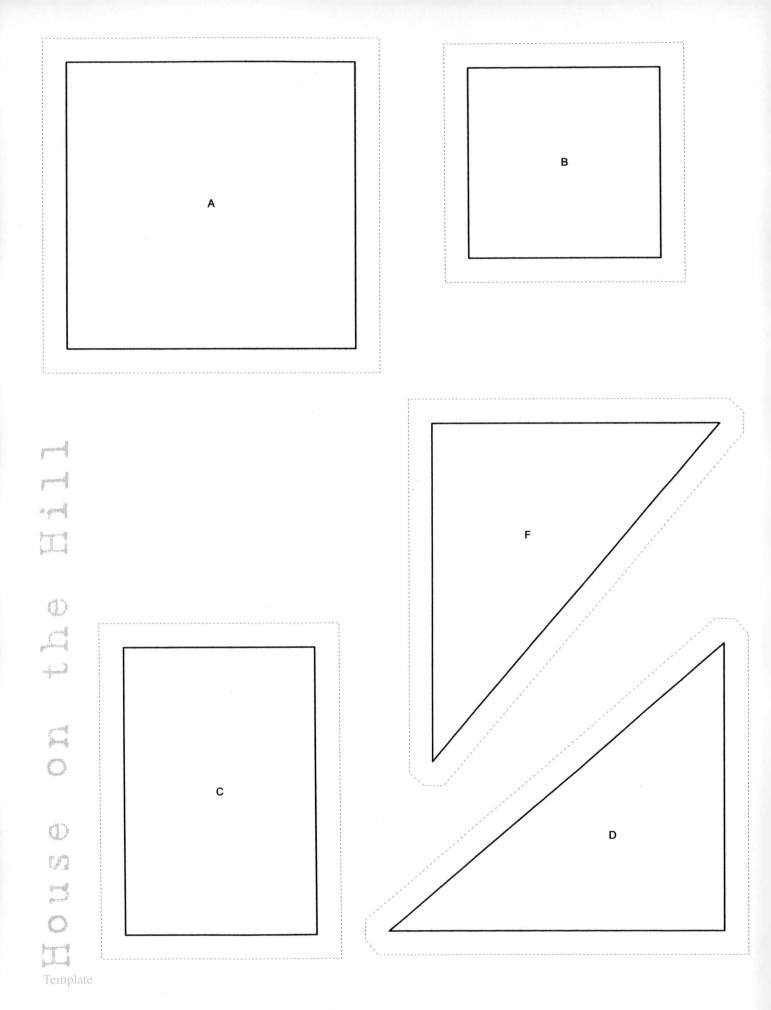

House on the Hill

Template

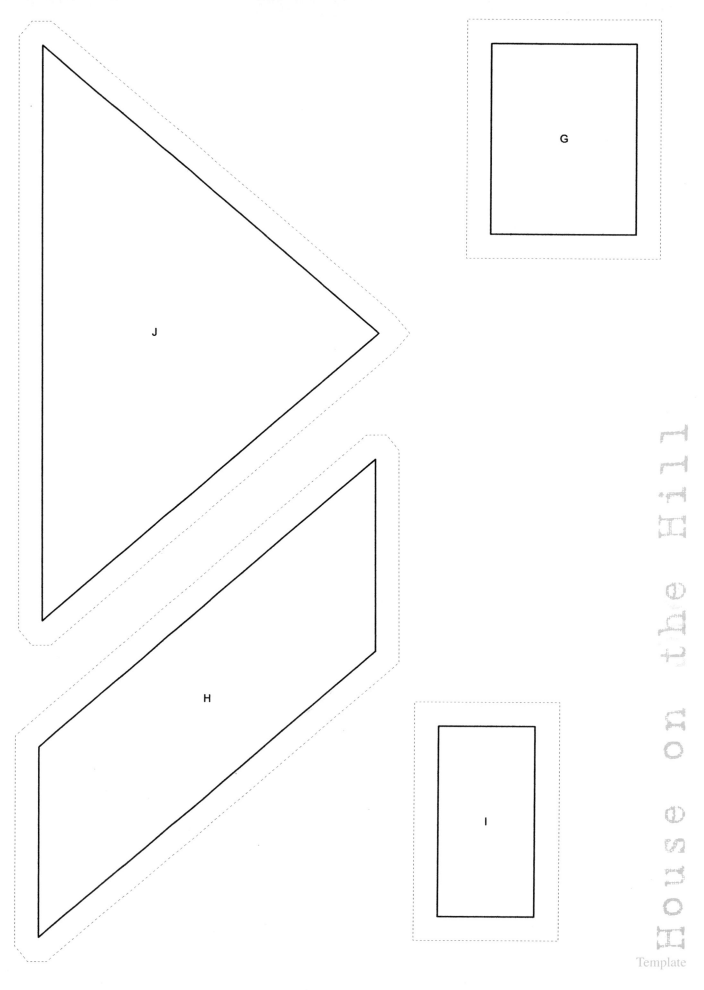

G

J

H

I

Template

White Lily

Block Size: 12" finished

Fabric Needed

Scraps of different whites

Dark blue

Green

Cutting Directions

From the dark blue fabric, cut

4 - 4" squares (Template A)

1 - 6 1/4" square. Cut the square twice on the diagonal or cut 3 triangles using Template B. (If you cut the square you will have one triangle left over.)

1 piece using Template C

From the white fabric, cut

3 diamonds using Template D

3 diamonds using Template E

From the green fabric, cut

1 leaf using Template G

1 stem using Template F

To Make the Block

1
Sew four of the white diamonds together in pairs as shown.

2
Inset a blue A square as shown to the two pairs of diamonds.

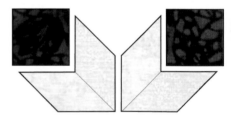

3
Inset a blue B triangle and stitch the units together.

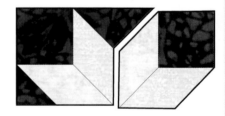

4
Appliqué the F stem to the C piece. Sew a diamond to either side of the top of piece C.

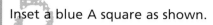

5 Inset a blue A square as shown.

6 Sew the top of the block to the bottom and inset the two remaining B triangles.

7 Appliqué the leaf in place to complete the block.

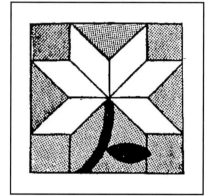

From The Kansas City Star,
February 8, 1936:
Number 441

The White Lily pattern was contributed by Miss Vernetta Plummar, Brumley, Mo. She points out this block can be pieced in two ways - by patching together the whole 9-inch square and using all the pieces, or by putting the six diamond-shaped petals together and appliqueing them on the square.

History of the Block

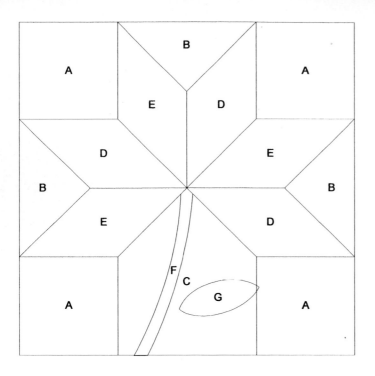

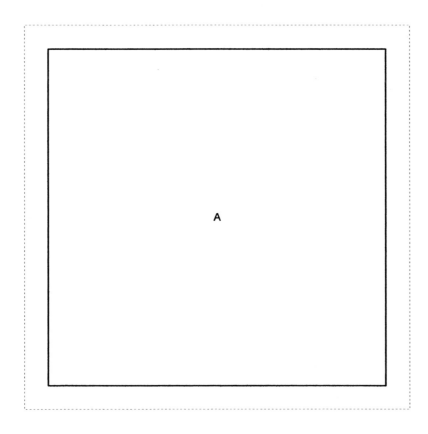

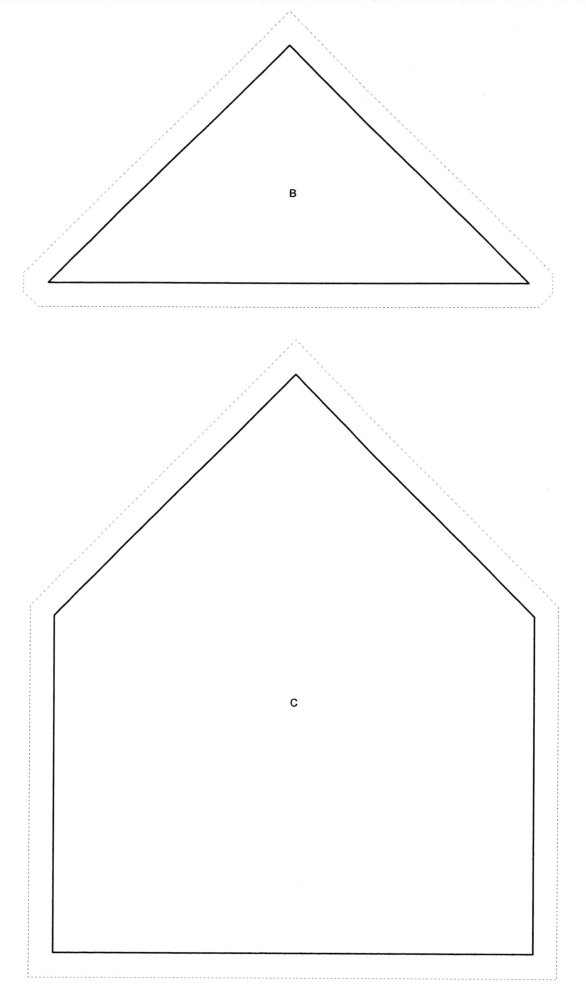

B

C

White Lily

Template

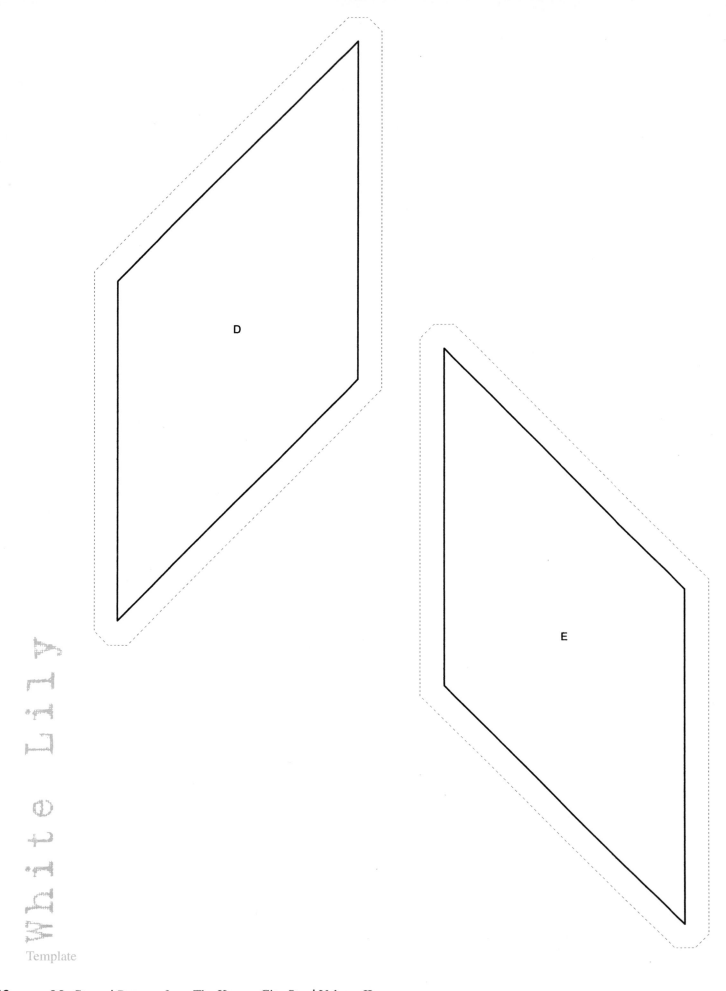

White Lily

Template

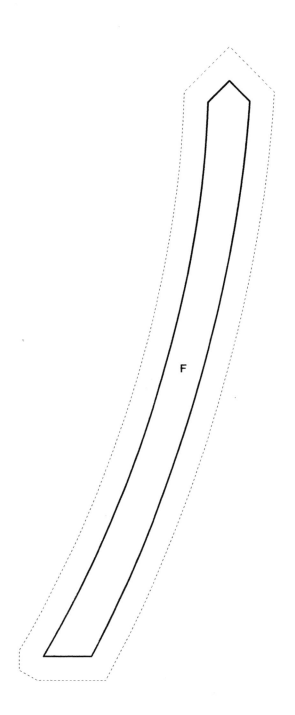

G

White Lily

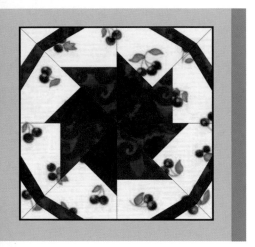

Crazy Anne

Block Size: 12" finished

Fabric Needed:

Dark green

Red

Red, green and white background print

Cutting Directions

From the red fabric, cut

4 triangles using template H

4 pieces using template E

From the green fabric, cut

4 triangles using template G

4 pieces using template B

From the background print, cut

4 pieces using template D

4 pieces using template C

4 pieces using template A

4 pieces using template F

To Make the Block

1 Sew a dark green G triangle to a background D piece. Add the red E piece, then the background F triangle. Make four of these units.

2 Sew a red H triangle to a background C piece. Then add a green B piece. Sew on the A triangle. Make four of these units.

3 Sew the units together into pairs to make up one quarter of the block.

Sew the block together as shown.

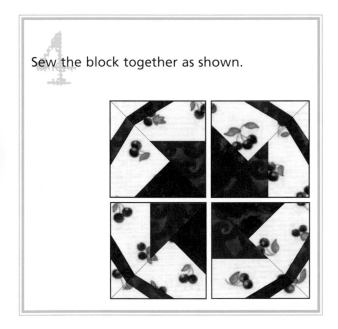

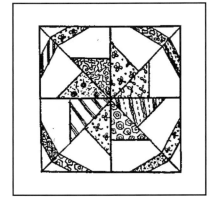

From The Kansas City Star,

June 15, 1949:

Number 264

Very distinctive is this quilt block with its whorl of prints accented by 1-tone pieces.

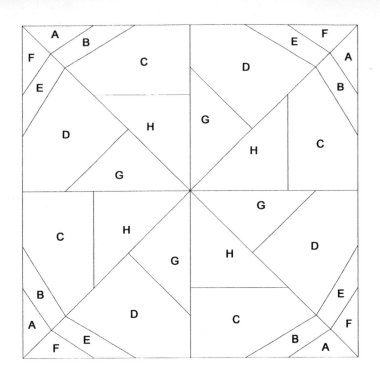

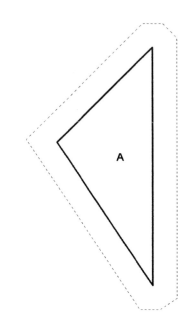

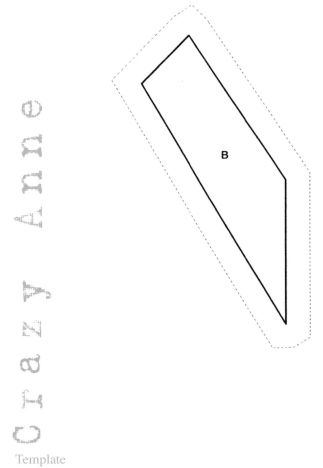

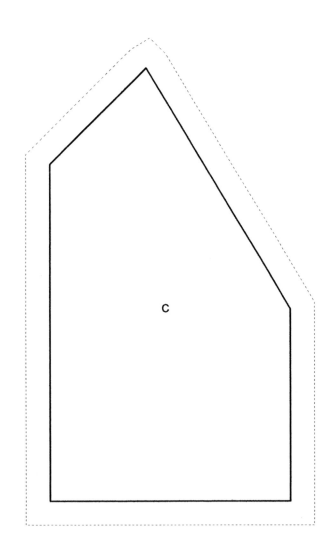

Crazy Anne

Template

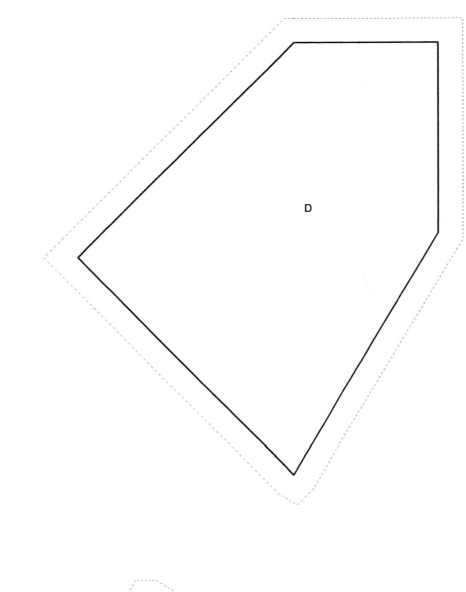

D

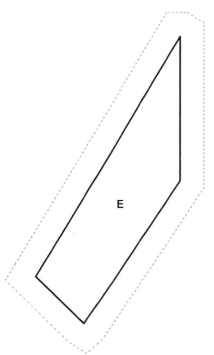

E

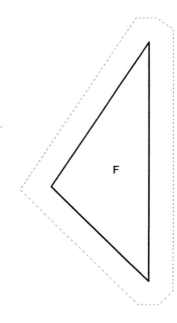

F

Template

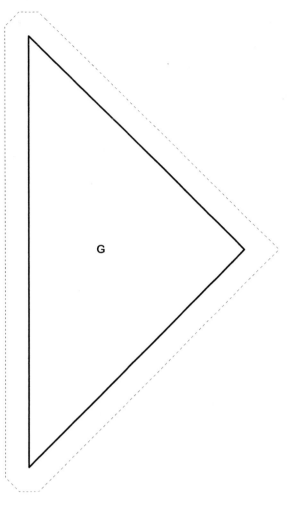

G

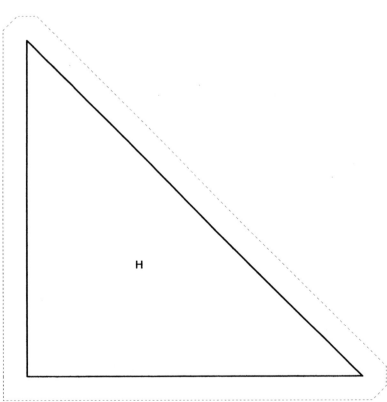

H

Template

Crazy Anne repaired and owned by Connie Wells, Rutherford, N.C. Original quilter unknown.

Sickle

Block Size: 12" finished

Fabric Needed:

Light green

Medium olive-green

Dark olive-green

Cutting Directions

From the dark olive-green fabric, cut

1 – 6 7/8" square or 2 triangles

using template A.

2 – 3 1/2" squares (template B)

From the light green fabric, cut

4 – 3 1/2" squares (template B)

From the medium olive-green fabric, cut

1 – 6 7/8" square or 2 triangles

using template A.

2 – 3 1/2" squares (template B)

To Make the Block

Draw a line from corner to corner on the diagonal on the reverse side of the medium olive-green 6 7/8" square. Place the medium green square atop the dark green square with right sides facing and sew 1/4" on either side of the line. Using your rotary cutter, cut on the marked line. Open the half-square triangle units and press toward the dark fabric. You should have 2 half-square triangles.

If you chose to cut the triangles using template A, sew the medium and dark green triangles together to make 2 half-square triangles.

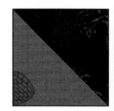

Sew the medium and light green squares together to make a four-patch unit.

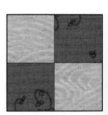

Sew the dark green and the light green squares together to make a four-patch unit.

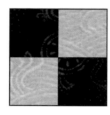

Sew the half-square triangles and the four-patch units together as shown to complete the block.

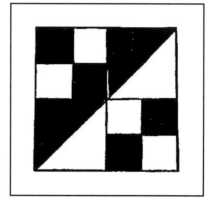

From The Kansas City Star, May 30, 1936:

Number 457

This block may be developed into a lovely quilt, featuring dark and light pieces. The pattern was contributed by Miss Prairie Wells, Moorewood, Ok.

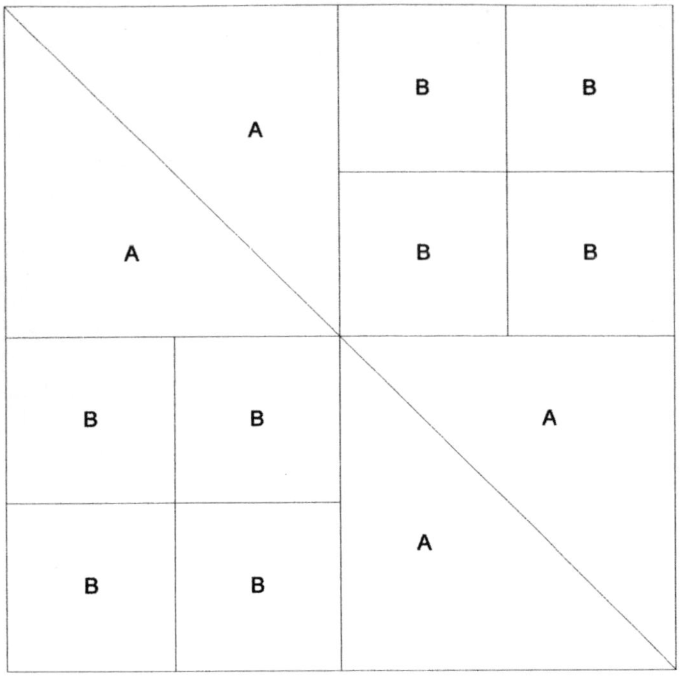

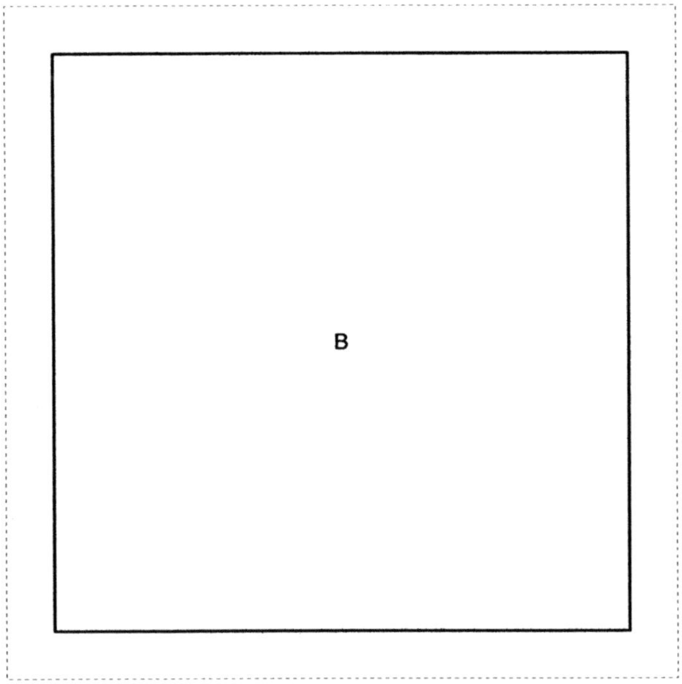

Sickle

Template

A

Sickle

Template

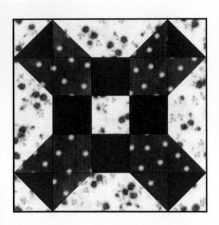

Fool's Square

Block Size: 12" finished

Fabric Needed:

Red and white background print

Red with white polka dots

Red

Cutting Directions

From the background print, cut

1 – 2 7/8" square (template C)

2 – 3 1/4" squares or 4 triangles

using template A

4 pieces using template B

From the red fabric, cut

4 – 2 7/8" squares (template C)

2 – 3 1/4" squares or 4 triangles

using template A

From the red dotted fabric, cut

4 – 2 7/8" squares (template C)

4 – 3 1/4" squares or 8 triangles

using template A

To Make the Block

1 If using squares instead of templates, take a scant 1/4" seam allowance so finished block will be 12" square.

If you cut squares from the red and background print fabrics, draw a line from corner to corner on the diagonal on the reverse side of the background fabric. Place a background square atop a red square with right sides facing and sew 1/4" on either side of the line. Using your rotary cutter, cut on the line. Open each of the half-square triangle units and press toward the darker fabric.

If you chose to cut the triangles using template A, sew the red and background triangles together to make 4 half-square triangles.

2 Sew a red dotted triangle to each end of piece B. Make four like this.

3 Sew the C squares together as shown in a 9-patch formation for the center of the block.

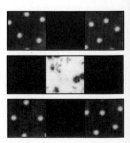

3 Sew the block together in rows as shown.

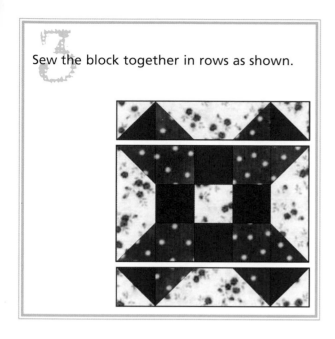

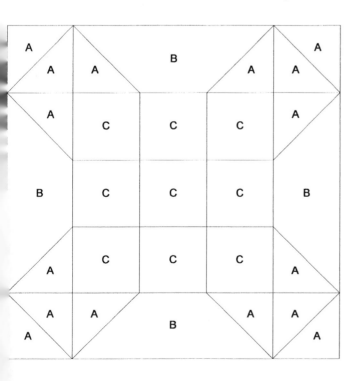

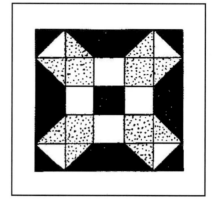

From The Kansas City Star,

July 5, 1955:

Number 952

This design was found by Mrs. May Bess, route 1, box 78, Poplar Bluff, Mo., in a scrapbook collection of her mother.

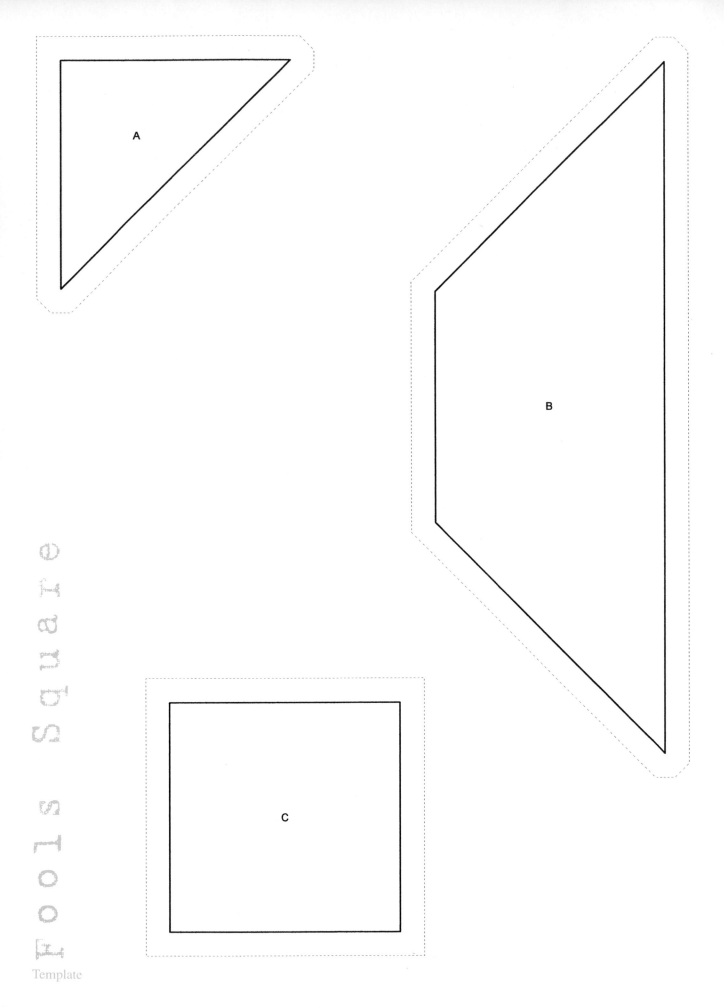

A

B

C

Fools Square

Template

Appeared in The Star **October 22, 1930**

To Make the Block

1 Sew the green print A triangles to the ivory hexagons.

2 Sew the red polka dot triangles onto the green and red striped hexagons.

3 Sew the red polka dot triangles onto the green and red striped hexagons.

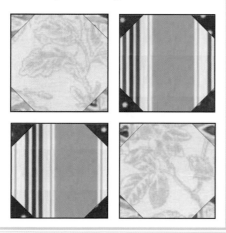

Marble Floor

Block size: 12" finished

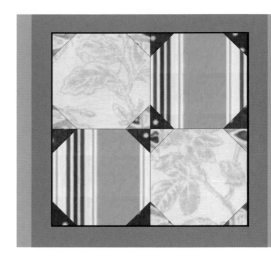

Fabric Needed:

Ivory

Green stripe

Red with white polka dots

Green and red print

Cutting Directions

From the green striped fabric, cut

2 hexagons using template B

From the ivory fabric, cut

2 hexagons using template B

From the green print, cut

8 triangles using template A

From the red and white polka dot fabric, cut

8 triangles using template A

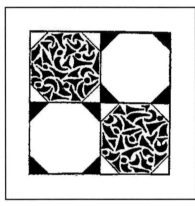

From The Kansas City Star,

October 22, 1930:

Number 127

"The Marble Floor" quilt pattern, another interesting design, is an easy one to make, but looks quite elaborate when finished. The four corner pieces are added to each large octagon and the block can then be pieced in rows. It is pretty either in solid colors or when figured fabrics are used as illustrated here. The finished block is ten inches square.

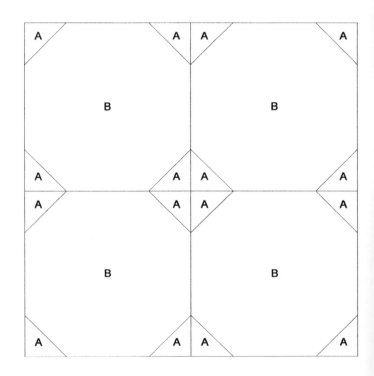

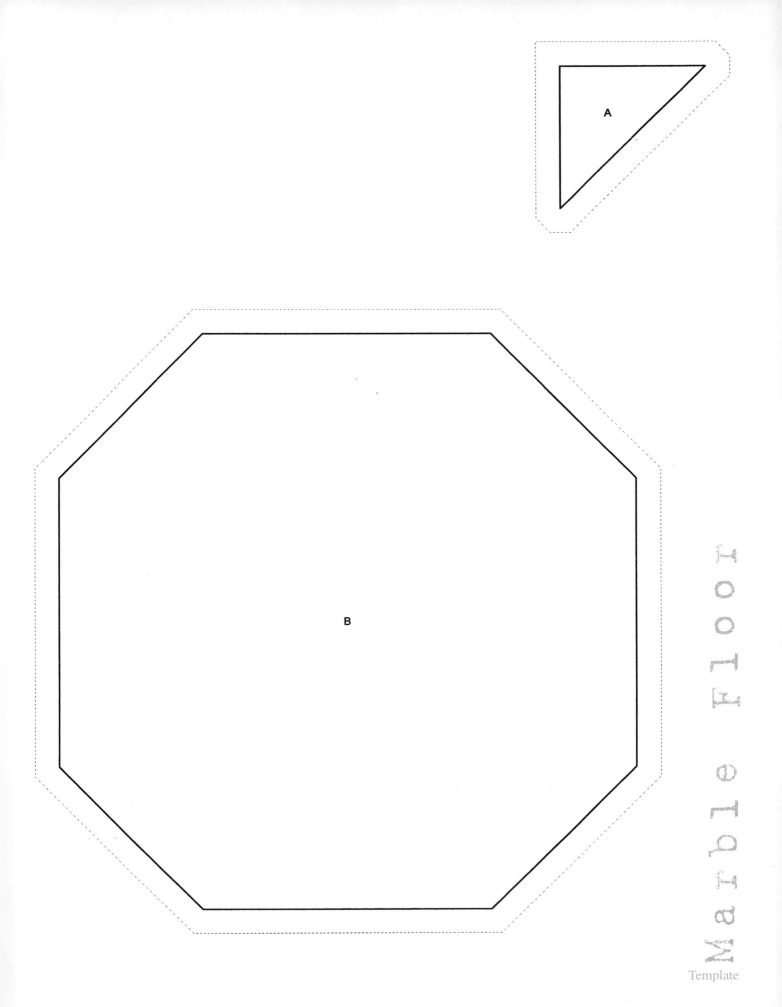

A

B

Marble Floor

Template

Snail Trail

Block Size: 12" finished

Fabric Needed:

2 Purples

2 Teals

Cutting Directions

From EACH of the four fabrics, cut

1 triangle using template A

1 triangle using template B

1 triangle using template C

1 triangle using template E

1 square using template D

NOTE:

As you sew the block together,

be very aware of your color placement.

To Make the Block

1

Sew the four squares together, making a four-patch for the center of the block.

2

Add the E triangles as shown.

3

Now sew on the B triangles.

4

Next add the C triangles. Be sure and check your color placement.

5

Sew on the A triangles to complete the block.

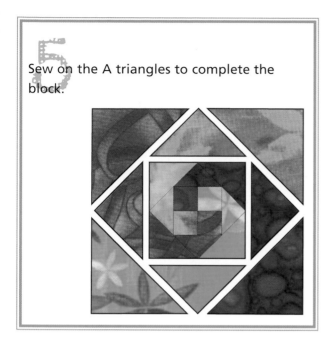

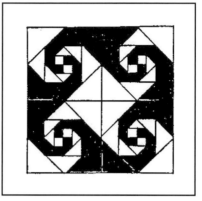

From The Kansas City Star,

November 16, 1935:

Number 429

Snail Trail is not as slow to complete as the name might suggest. The clever arrangement of square and triangular blocks gives a continuous-curve effect to the all-over design of the finished quilt. This pattern is the contribution of Vera B. Martin, Carthage, Mo.

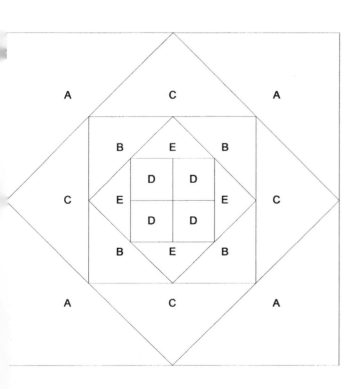

History of the Block

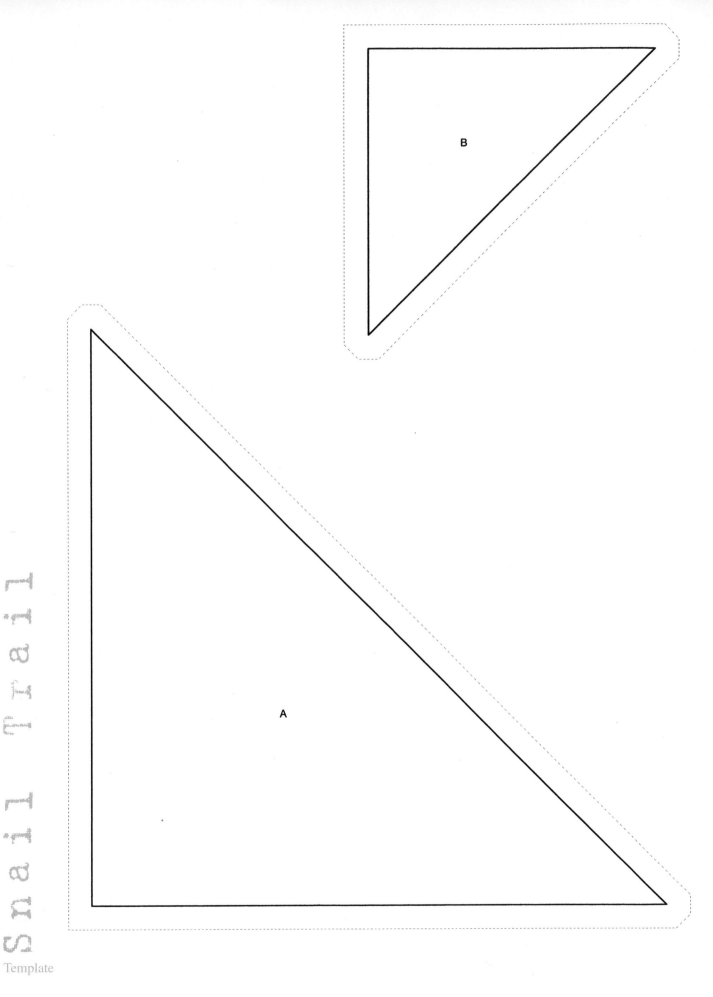

B

A

Snail Trail

Template

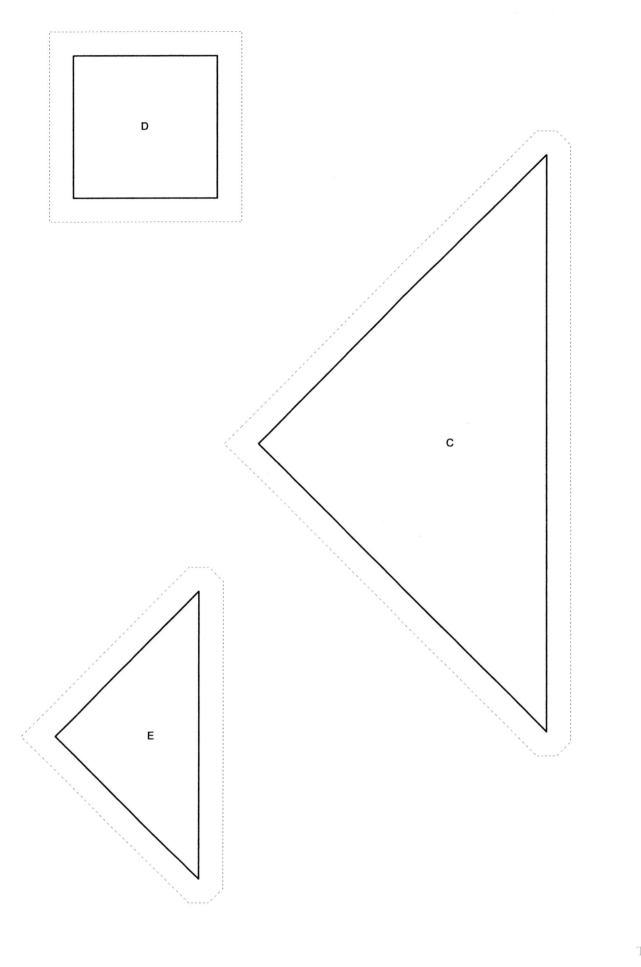

D

C

E

Snow Trail designed by Lynda Hall, Apopka, Fla. Quilted by The Old Green Cupboard, Jacksonville, Fla.

Appeared in The Star **April 5, 1950**

To Make the Block

Make two half-square triangle units by sewing the off white triangles to the light pink print triangles.

Sew four of the A triangles together as shown. Make two units like this.

Sew two green and one pink A triangles together as shown. Make four strips like this.

Make four corner units by sewing a light pink A triangle to an off white triangle as shown

Grandma's Hop-Scotch

Block Size: 12" finished

Fabric Needed:
Off white

Green

Light pink print

Dark pink print

Cutting Directions
From the green fabric, cut
3 – 5 1/14" squares. Cut each square from corner to corner twice on the diagonal making 12 triangles or cut 10 triangles using template A. (If you cut the squares, you will have two triangles left over).

From the dark pink print fabric, cut
1 – 5 1/4" square. Cut the square from corner to corner twice on the diagonal making 4 triangles or cut 2 triangles using template A. (If you cut the squares, you will have two triangles left over.)

From the light pink fabric, cut
3 – 5 1/4" squares. Cut each square from corner to corner twice on the diagonal making 12 triangles or cut 10 triangles using template A. (If you cut the squares, you will have two triangles left over.)

1 – 4 7/8" square. Cut the square once on the diagonal or cut 2 triangles using template B.

From the off white fabric, cut
2 – 5 1/4" squares. Cut each square twice on the diagonal making 8 triangles or cut 6 triangles using template A. (If you cut the squares, you will have two triangles left over.)

1 – 4 7/8" square. Cut the square once on the diagonal or cut 2 triangles using template B.

Grandma's Hop-Scotch

From The Kansas City Star,
April 5, 1950:
Number 870

Because she thinks other readers of The Weekly Star might be interested in making the Hop-Scotch quilt, Mrs. E. T. Delver, Stillwater, Ok., has contributed the pattern, which was a favorite with her grandmother. She accompanies the design with the following directions concerning yardage and assembling the blocks. "These 12-inch blocks should be set together without any intervening strips or plain blocks. Variety in the pattern is obtained by turning every other block so it faces the other way. Following is the yardage required: 2-3/4 yards orange, 2-1/2 yards brown, 4 yards yellow. A good size for the quilt is 80 by 92 inches. This will take thirty blocks; five across and six down, with a 10-inch border. The border requires three yards of yellow and the back of the quilt will take six yards. Thus, if the background of the blocks, the border and the back are all of the same material, it will total twelve and one-half yards of the yellow. The quilt may also be made in red, white and blue, or any other color scheme. Prints make a very pretty quilt also.

Make the center of the block first. Sew the half-square triangle units to the quarter-square triangles units as shown.

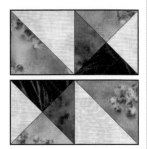

Sew the sides, top and bottom strips to the center of the block.

Add the corners to complete the block.

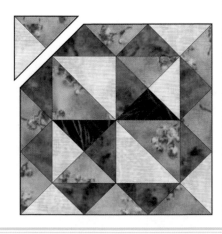

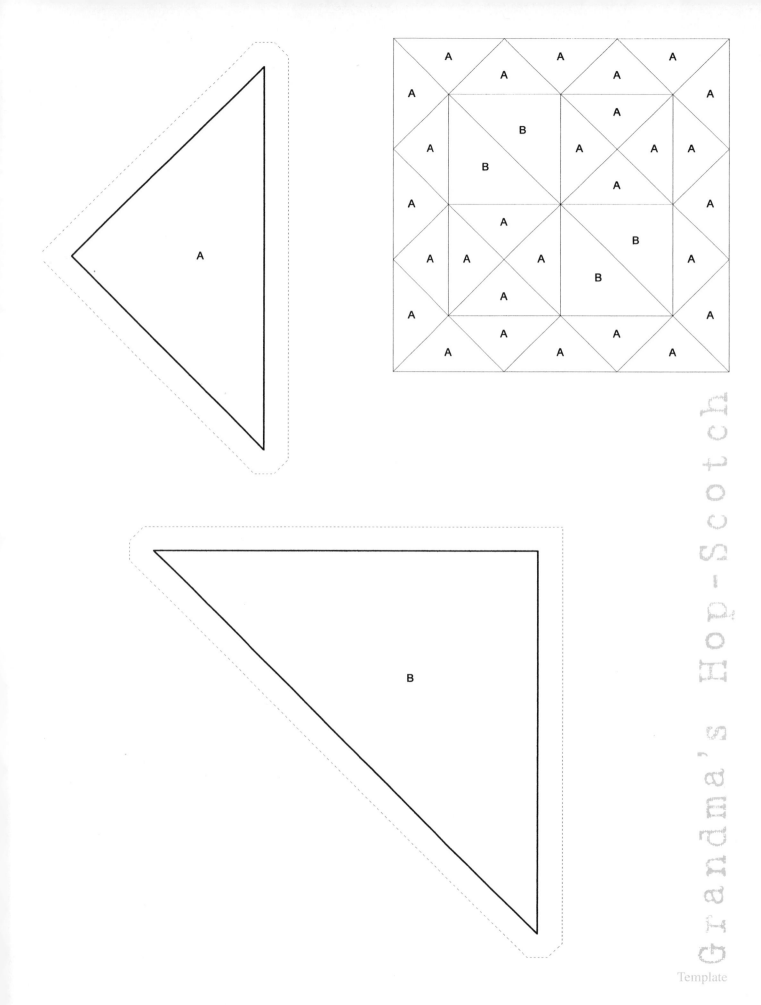

A

B

Template

Mexican Star

Block Size: 12" finished

Fabric Needed:

Tan

Medium purple

Dark purple

Cutting Directions

From the tan fabric, cut

1 - 7 1/4" square. Cut the square from corner to corner twice on the diagonal or cut 4 triangles using template C.

5 - 1 15/16" squares (template F)

4 - 2 7/8" squares. Cut each square from corner to corner once on the diagonal or cut 8 triangles using template B.

From the medium purple, cut

4 pieces using template D

4 pieces using template E

From the dark purple, cut

4 - 1 15/16" squares (template F)

4 pieces using template A

To Make the Block

We will sew this block together on the diagonal.

Sew the B triangles to the D and E pieces as shown.

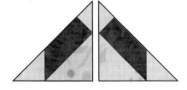

Sew the F squares together to make a nine-patch unit for the center of the block.

To make the upper right part of the block, sew a C triangle to the D and E pieces.

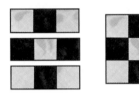

To make the upper right part of the block, sew a C triangle to the D and E pieces.

Mexican Star

Next make the center portion of the block. Sew the remaining B-D and B-E units to the A strips. You should have two units. Sew the two units to the center nine-patch.

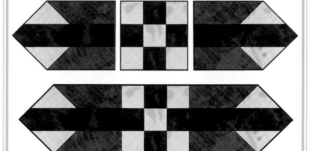

Sew the three rows together to complete the block.

**From The Kansas City Star,
July 5, 1930:**
Number 104

Recently a quilt collector found a beautiful old "Mexican Star" quilt up in the mountains of York state. It was a handsome specimen in red and blues. How these same lovely patterns are found North, South, East, and West testify of the far-flung ties that bound together the scattered settlers of Mexican War days, when this pattern was doubtless originated. This is rather an intricate pattern to piece, but the effect when set together as shown entirely of pieced blocks looks more beautiful than bewildering. If you are a quilt enthusiast, "Mexican Star" will tempt you. Seams are not allowed.

**From The Kansas City Star,
December 31, 1941:**
Number 672

From her collection of quilt block designs, Mrs. Melvin Nielsen, Boone, Colo., has lent the Mexican Star, a popular pattern, which was printed in The Weekly Star several years ago.

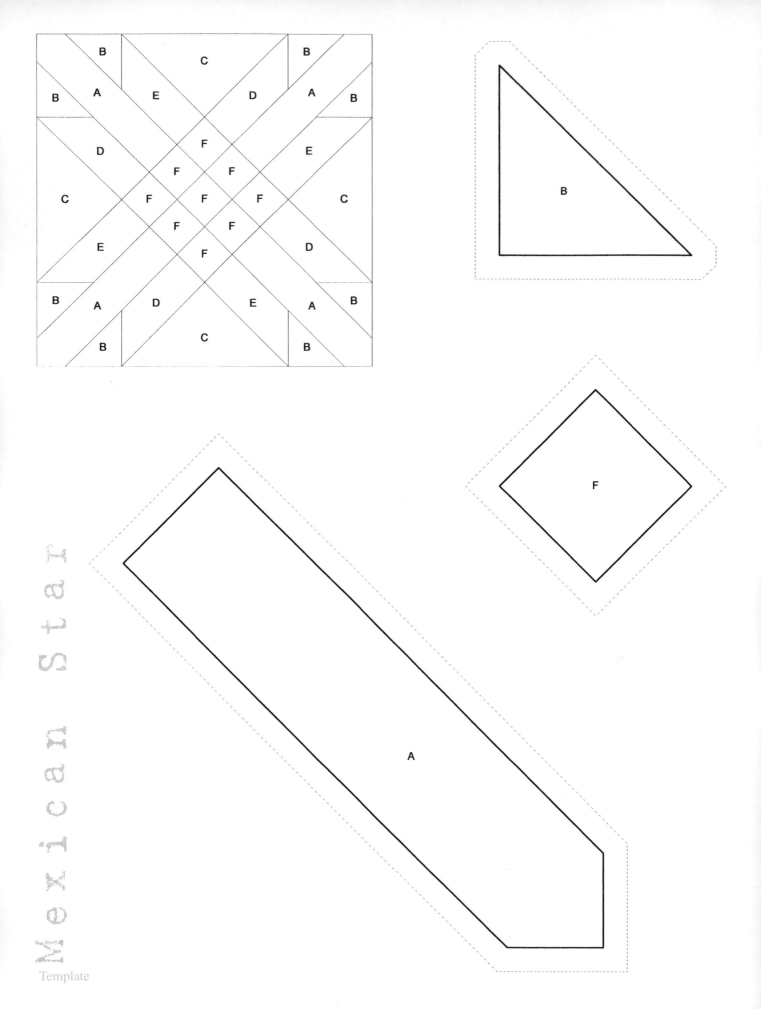

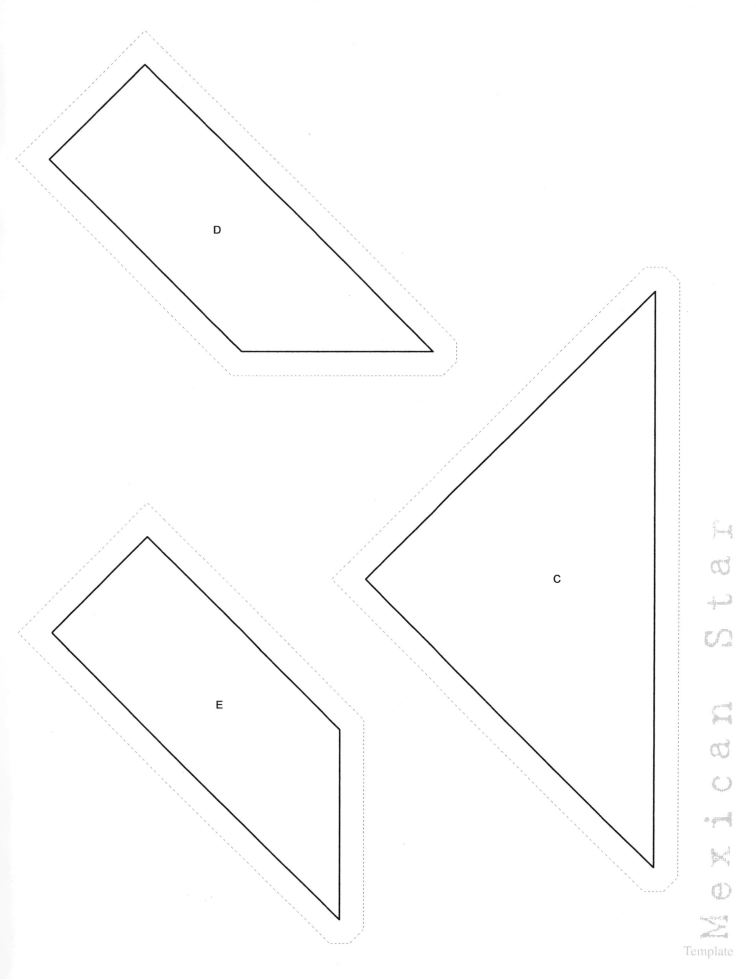

D

C

E

Mexican Star

Template

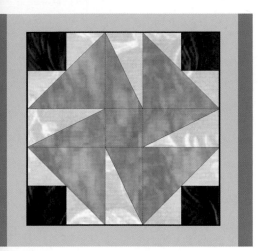

Crazy Anne

Block Size: 12" finished

Fabric Needed:

Dark orange

Light orange

Navy blue

Cutting Directions

From the navy blue fabric, cut

4 – 2 7/8" squares (template A)

From the light orange fabric, cut

4 – 3 1/4" squares. Cut each square once on the diagonal or cut 8 triangles using template B.

4 triangles using template C

From the dark orange fabric, cut

4 triangles using template C

1 – 2 7/8" square (template A)

2 - 5 5/8" squares. Cut each square once on the diagonal or cut 4 triangles using template D.

To Make the Block

1

If using squares instead of templates, take a scant 1/4" seam allowance so finished block will be 12" square.

Sew two light orange triangles to a blue square as shown. Then add a dark orange D triangle.

2

Stitch the dark orange and light orange C triangles together. You should have four units that look like this.

3

Sew the block together in rows as shown.

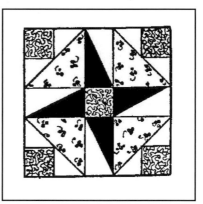

**From The Kansas City Star,
October 15, 1932:**
Number 855

This futuristic pattern is so prophetic of the latest trend in decorative design as to be quite startling, yet it is one of our great-grandmother's favorites. While three colors are shown above, two are equally interesting and give an entirely different effect. This is not a difficult block to piece as the rows are so well defined and the edges straight. It is twelve inches square and will be alternated with plain blocks of the same size. No seams are allowed.

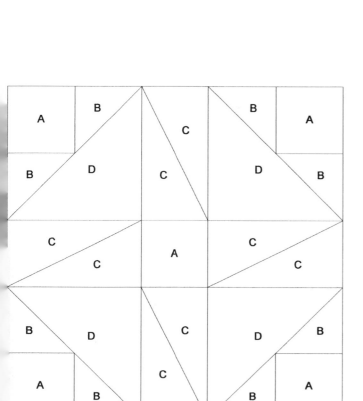

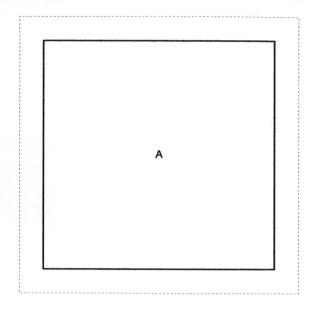

A

Crazy Anne

Template

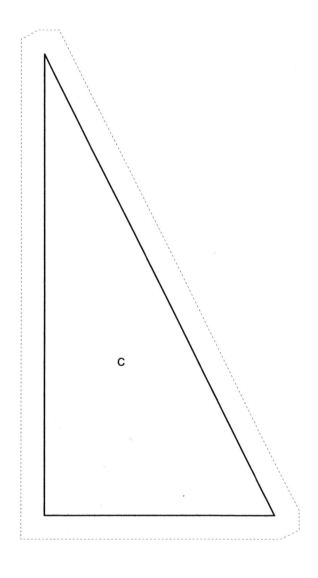

C

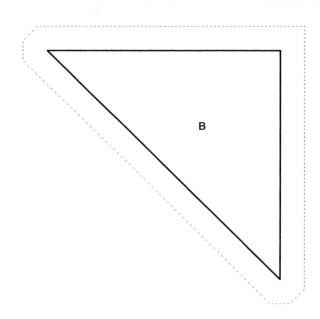

B

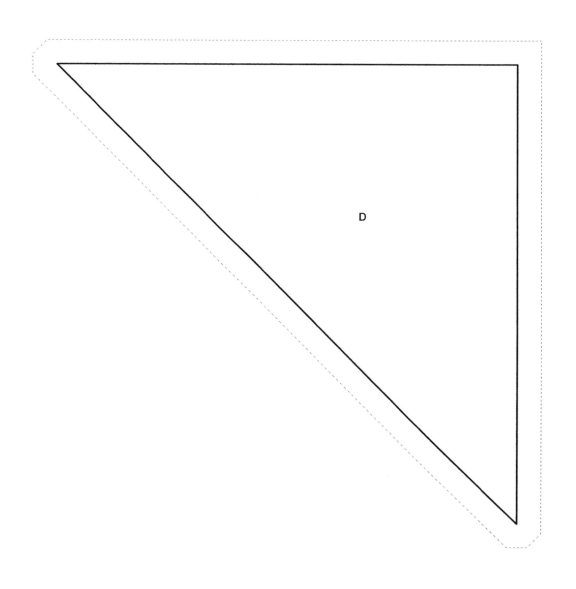

D

Crazy Anne

Template

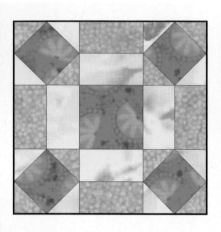

Squirrel in a Cage

Block Size: 12" finished

Appeared in The Star **November 2, 1935**

Fabric Needed:

Green and yellow print

Dark green print

Light green print

Cutting Directions

From the dark green print, cut

4 - 3 5/16" squares (template D)

1 - 4 1/2" square (template C)

From the light green print, cut

4 - 4 1/2" x 2 1/2" rectangles (Template B)

4 - 2 7/8" squares. Cut the squares from corner

to corner once on the diagonal, making

8 triangles or cut 8 triangles using template A.

From the green and yellow print, cut

4 - 4 1/2" x 2 1/2" rectangles (Template B)

4 - 2 7/8" squares. Cut the squares from corner

to corner once on the diagonal, making

8 triangles or cut 8 triangles using template A.

To Make the Block

1 Sew the green and yellow print rectangles to the light green rectangles. Make four.

2 Make four corner units by sewing a light green triangle to opposing sides of the dark green D square. Now add a yellow and green print triangle to the remaining two sides of the square. Make four.

Squirrel in a Cage

Sew the units together into rows as shown below. Then sew the rows together to complete the block.

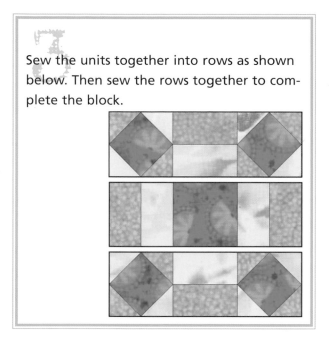

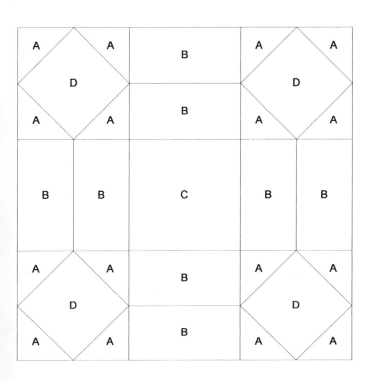

From The Kansas City Star,

November 2, 1935:

Number 427

"Squirrel in a Cage" is a quilt which many quilt makers may remember seeing their mothers and grandmothers make. Mrs. Mary K. Rogers, Manhattan, Kas., copied this pattern from a quilt made by her mother many years ago.

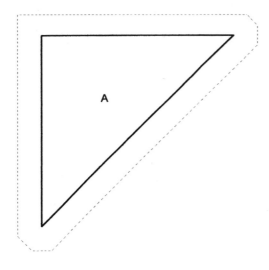

A

C

Template

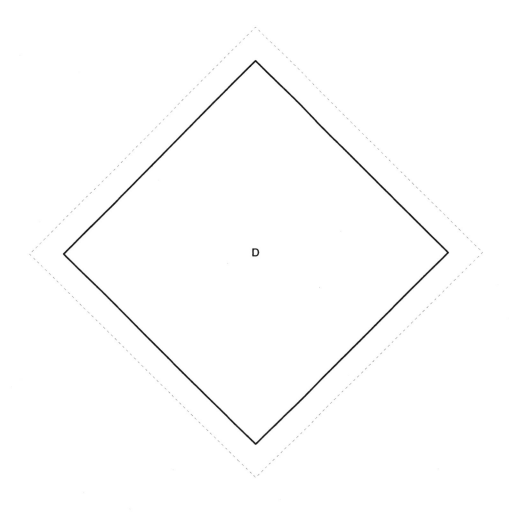

Template

Modern Envelope

Block Size: 12" finished

Modern Envelope

Fabric Needed:

Light tan
Medium blue
Dark blue

Cutting Directions

From the light tan, cut

1 - 7 1/4" square. Cut the square twice from corner to corner on the diagonal to make 4 triangles or cut 4 triangles using template B.

From the dark blue, cut

1 - 7 1/4" square. Cut the square twice from corner to corner on the diagonal to make 4 triangles or cut 4 triangles using template B.

From the medium blue, cut

2 - 6 7/8" squares. Cut each square once on the diagonal from corner to corner or cut 4 triangles using template A.

To Make the Block

1
Sew a dark blue B triangle to a light tan B triangle. Then add an A triangle. Make four units like this.

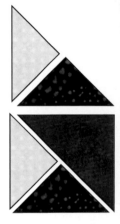

2
Sew the four units together as shown to complete the block.

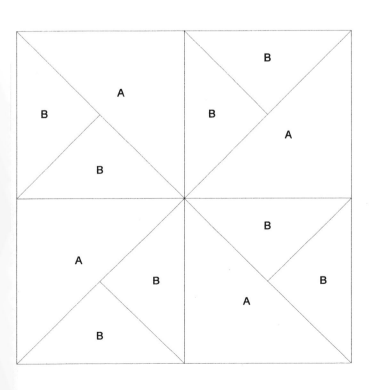

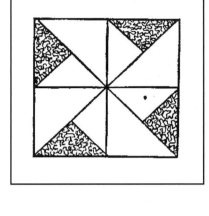

From The Kansas City Star,

September 26, 1945:

Number 774

Harmonizing contrasts for the two sizes of 1-tone blocks are suggested for this pattern, which was designed by Miss Pearl Hursh, Rueter, Mo.

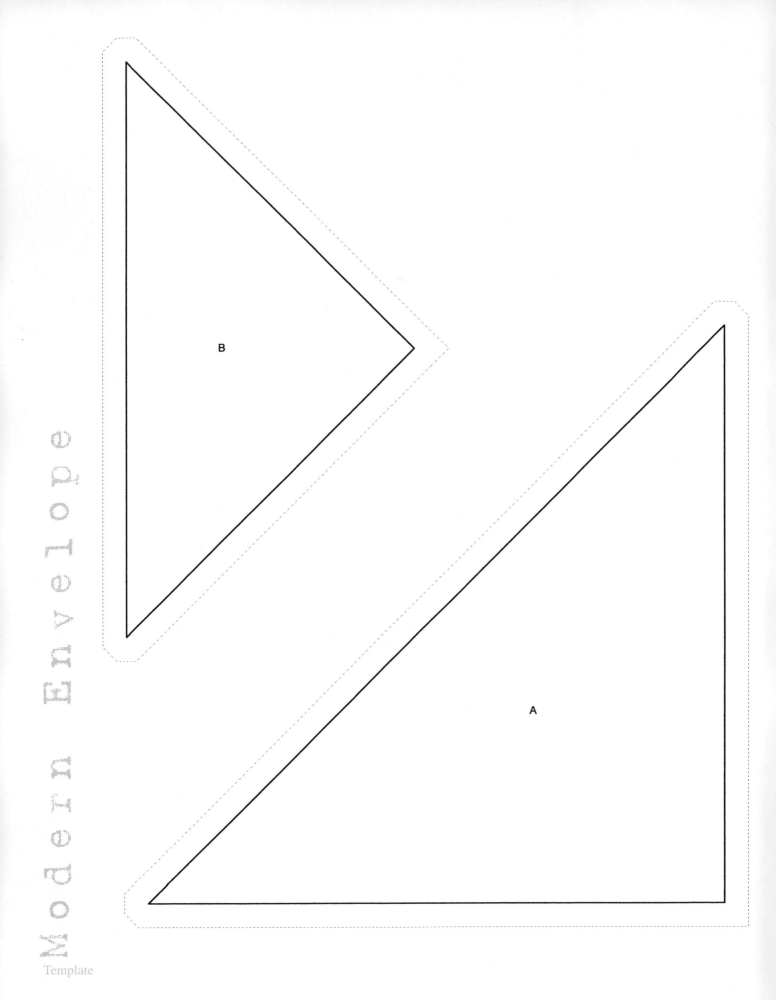

B

A

Template

Wind Magic designed and quilted by Judy Laquidara, Nevada, Mo.

Whirling Star

Block Size: 12" finished

Appeared in The Star **January 30, 1937**

Take particular notice of the way this 8-pointed star is constructed. Four of the points are made with the pieces sewn together like the following diagram.

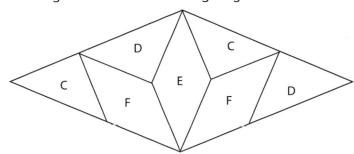

The other four points are made with the pieces sewn together in this order.

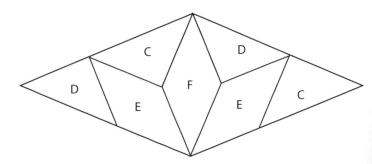

Fabric Needed

Black

Red

Tan

Cutting Directions

From the black fabric, cut

4 – 4" squares (Template A)

1 – 6 3/16" square. Cut the square

twice on the diagonal or

cut 4 triangles using Template B.

From the red fabric, cut

12 diamonds using Template E

12 diamonds using Template F

From the light tan fabric, cut

16 triangles using Template C

16 triangles using Template D

To Make the Block

For the first set of points, sew the three red diamonds together. You'll use pieces F-E-F. Add piece C and D. Then inset piece D and C as shown. Make 4.

For the second set of points, sew 3 red diamonds together in the following order, E-F-E. Add piece C and D. Then inset piece C and D. Make 4.

Sew 4 star points together. Begin with one point from the first set, then add a point from the second set. Alternate the points. Make two sets like this. You now have the two halves that make up the star. Press the seams so they go in a counterclockwise direction.

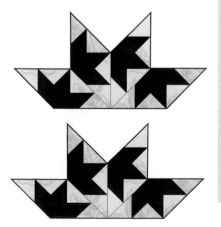

Sew the two halves together making sure the seams in the center of the star butt perfectly.

Inset the black A squares on the corners of the block. Inset the B triangles to complete the block.

From The Kansas City Star,

January 30, 1937:

Number 488

This lovely quilt block has a star motif that demands skill and accuracy in piecing. This quilt may be set together with strips or in an all-over pattern. The pattern was contributed by Mrs. Harold Fann, Waverly, Kansas.

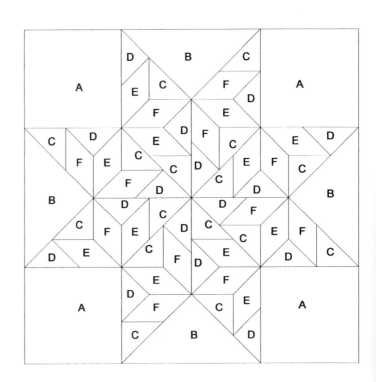

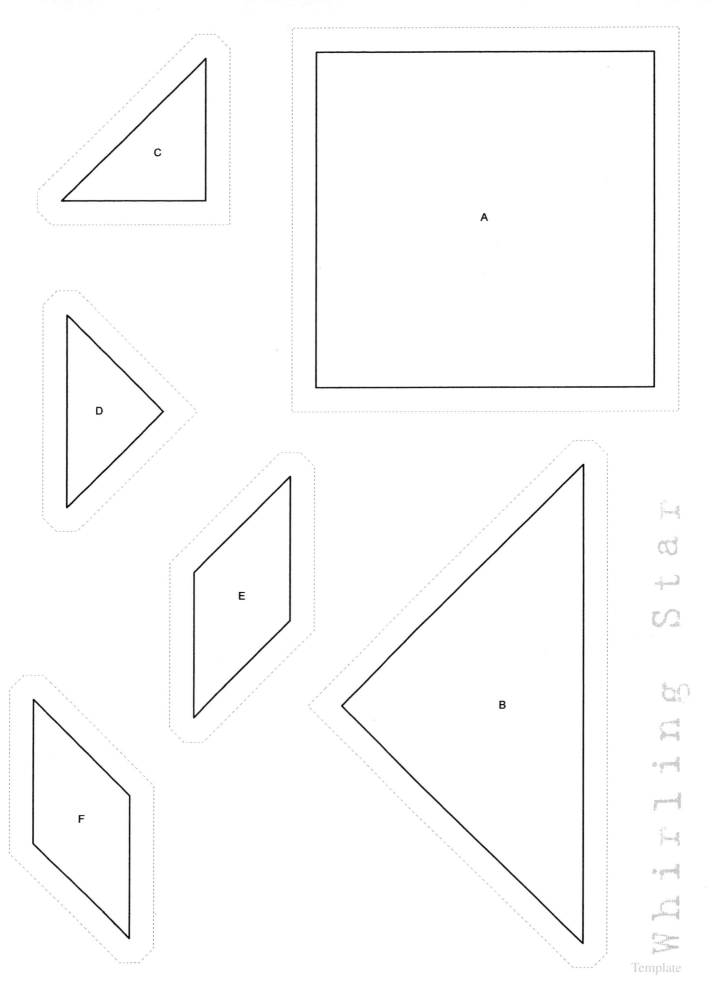

C

A

D

E

B

F

Whirling Star

Template

Posey

Block Size: 12" finished

Fabric Needed:

Green
Pink print
Yellow
Dark pink
Tan

Cutting Directions

From the tan background fabric, cut

2 – 6 7/8" squares. Cut each square once on the diagonal or cut 4 triangles using template A.
1 piece using template C

From the green fabric, cut

4 stems using template D
4 leaves using template F
4 leaves using template G

From the yellow fabric, cut

4 circles using template E

From the dark pink fabric, cut

4 circles using template H

From the pink print fabric, cut

4 pieces using template B

To Make the Block

1

Do the appliqué work before piecing the block.

Fold the A triangles in half and gently finger-press a crease into the fabric. Be careful not to stretch the bias edge. Center the stems on the creases and match up the bottom edge of the stem with the edge of the triangle and pin in place.

Appliqué the flowers, flower centers, leaves and stems in place using your favorite method.

2

Sew the pink print B pieces to the center C piece. Sew the appliquéd triangles in place to complete the block.

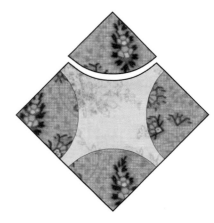

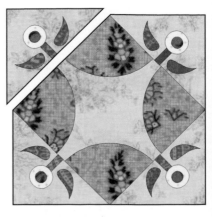

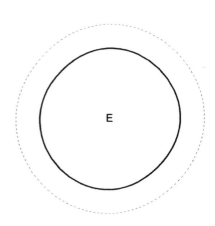

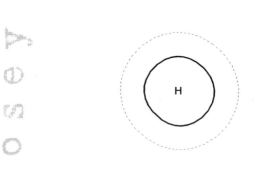

Posey Template

From The Kansas City Star, June 8, 1929:
Number 38

In answer to many requests, we have had a pattern made of the posey quilt which was in one of The Star's exhibition homes. It is a combination of patchwork and applique. A small pink flower with a yellow center and green stem is appliqued on each of the largest white triangles. These form the four corners of the block. The large center patch must be cut on a fold of material as indicated in the pattern. Four blue triangles fit into the sides of the center block. These quilt blocks are put together with alternating white blocks set diagonally. An attractive border is indicated in the sketch, being made of two strips of the blue a half-inch wide with the flower motif appliqued at intervals. When cutting your pieces, be sure to allow for seams.

History of the Block

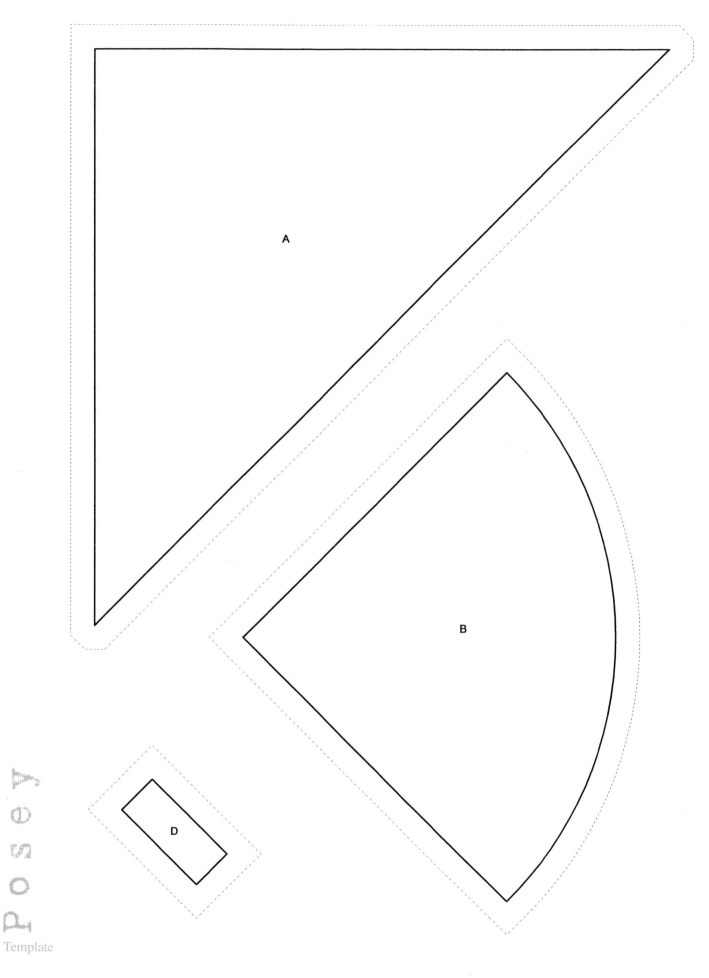

A

B

D

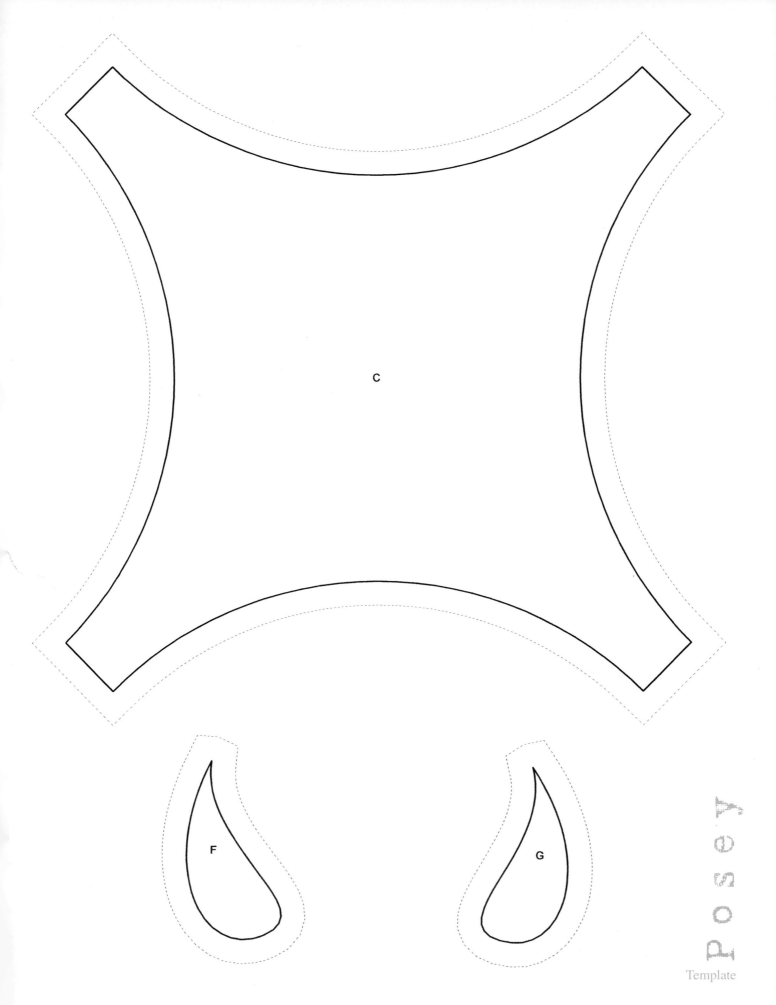

C

F

G

Posey

Template

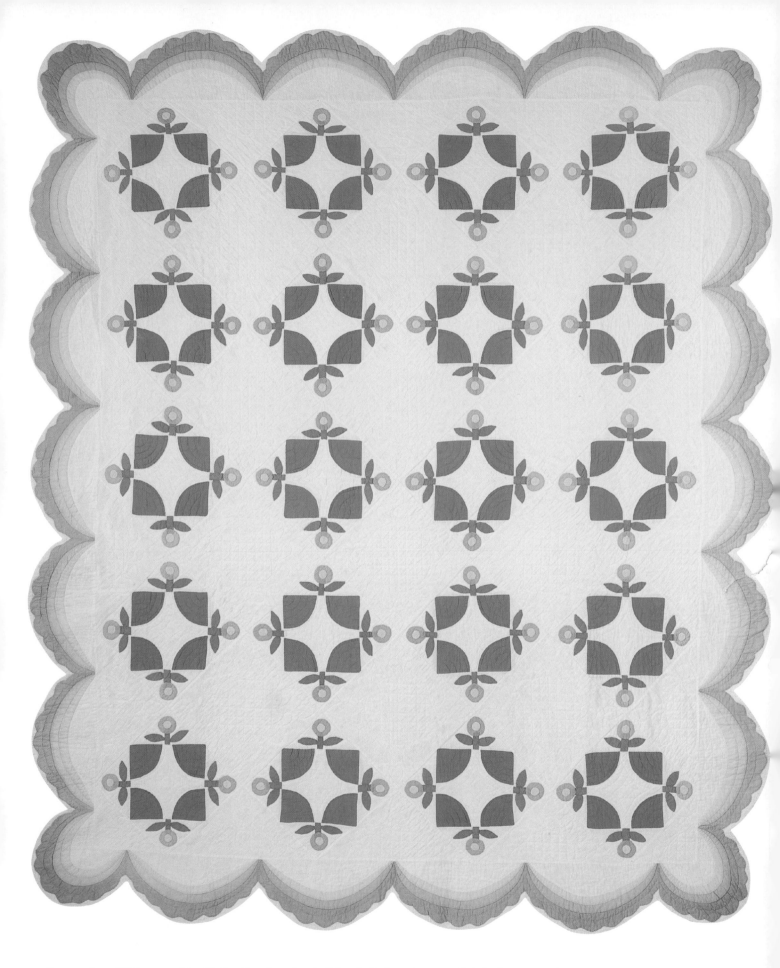

Posey, circa 1935, owned by Kathy Kansier, Ozark, Mo., kathykansier.com. Original owner unknown.

Appeared in The Star **October 26, 1938**

Flying X
Block Size: 12" finished

To Make the Block

1

If you cut squares from the tan and blue fabrics, draw a line from corner to corner on the diagonal on the reverse side of the tan fabric. Place a tan square atop a blue square with right sides facing and sew 1/4" on either side of the line. Using your rotary cutter, cut on the line. Open each of the half-square triangle units and press toward the dark fabric.

If you chose to cut the triangles using template B, sew the tan and blue triangles together to make 8 half-square triangles.

2

Sew the squares and half-square triangle units into rows as shown.

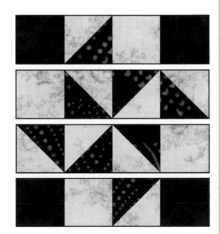

Sew the rows together to complete the block.

Fabric Needed:

Red

Tan

Navy blue

Cutting Directions
From the red fabric, cut

4 - 3 1/2" squares (template A)

From the tan fabric, cut

4 - 3 1/2" squares (template A)

4 - 3 7/8" squares or 8 triangles using template B

From the navy blue fabric, cut

4 - 3 7/8" squares or 8 triangles using template B

From The Kansas City Star,

October 26, 1938:

Number 562

The finished block of Flying X looks intricate, but the piecing of the block is simple. The pattern was contributed by Mrs. Lizzie Robinson, Anderson, Mo. Thank you.

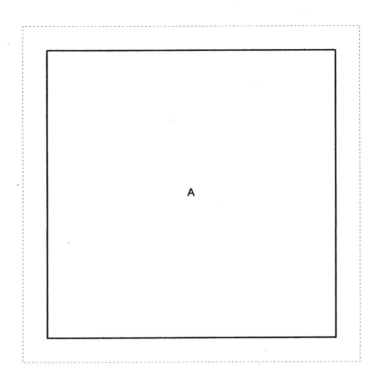

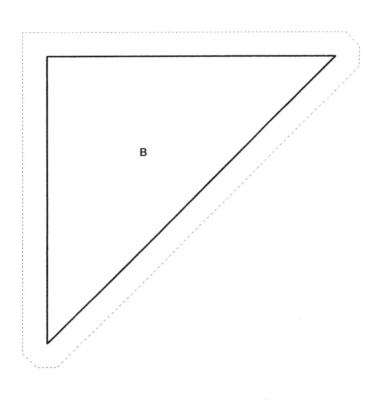

Flying X

Template

Other Star Books

One Piece at a Time by Kansas City Star Books – 1999

More Kansas City Star Quilts by Kansas City Star Books – 2000

Outside the Box: Hexagon Patterns from The Kansas City Star by Edie McGinnis – 2001

Prairie Flower: A Year on the Plains by Barbara Brackman – 2001

The Sister Blocks by Edie McGinnis – 2001

Kansas City Quiltmakers by Doug Worgul – 2001

O' Glory: Americana Quilts Blocks from The Kansas City Star by Edie McGinnis – 2001

Hearts and Flowers: Hand Appliqué from Start to Finish by Kathy Delaney – 2002

Roads and Curves Ahead: A Trip Through Time with Classic Kansas City Star Quilt Blocks by Edie McGinnis – 2002

Celebration of American Life: Appliqué Patterns Honoring a Nation and Its People by Barb Adams and Alma Allen – 2002

Women of Grace & Charm: A Quilting Tribute to the Women Who Served in World War II by Barb Adams and Alma Allen – 2003

A Heartland Album: More Techniques in Hand Appliqué by Kathy Delaney – 2003

Quilting a Poem: Designs Inspired by America's Poets by Frances Kite and Deb Rowden – 2003

Carolyn's Paper Pieced Garden: Patterns for Miniature and Full-Sized Quilts by Carolyn Cullinan McCormick – 2003

Friendships in Bloom: Round Robin Quilts by Marjorie Nelson and Rebecca Nelson-Zerfas – 2003

Baskets of Treasures: Designs Inspired by Life Along the River by Edie McGinnis – 2003

Heart & Home: Unique American Women and the Houses that Inspire by Kathy Schmitz – 2003

Women of Design: Quilts in the Newspaper by Barbara Brackman – 2004

The Basics: An Easy Guide to Beginning Quiltmaking by Kathy Delaney – 2004

Four Block Quilts: Echoes of History, Pieced Boldly & Appliquéd Freely by Terry Clothier Thompson – 2004

No Boundaries: Bringing Your Fabric Over the Edge by Edie McGinnis – 2004

Horn of Plenty for a New Century by Kathy Delaney – 2004

Quilting the Garden by Barb Adams and Alma Allen – 2004

Stars All Around Us: Quilts and Projects Inspired by a Beloved Symbol by Cherie Ralston – 2005

Quilters' Stories: Collecting History in the Heart of America by Deb Rowden – 2005

Libertyville: Where Liberty Dwells, There is My Country by Terry Clothier Thompson – 2005

Sparkling Jewels, Pearls of Wisdom by Edie McGinnis – 2005

Grapefruit Juice and Sugar: Bold Quilts Inspired by Grandmother's Legacy by Jenifer Dick – 2005

Home Sweet Home by Barb Adams and Alma Allen – 2005

Patterns of History: The Challenge Winners by Kathy Delaney – 2005

My Quilt Stories by Debra Rowden – 2005

Quilts in Red and Green and the Women Who Made Them by Nancy Hornback and Terry Clothier Thompson – 2006

Hard Times, Splendid Quilts: A 1930s Celebration, Paper Piecing from The Kansas City Star by Carolyn Cullinan McCormick – 2006

Art Nouveau Quilts for the 21st Century by Bea Oglesby – 2006

Designer Quilts: Great Projects from Moda's Best Fabric Artists – 2006

Birds of a Feather by Barb Adams and Alma Allen – 2006

Feedsacks! Beautiful Quilts from Humble Beginnings by Edie McGinnis – 2006

Kansas Spirit: Historical Quilt Blocks and the Saga of the Sunflower State by Jeanne Poore – 2006

Bold Improvisation: Searching for African-American Quilts – The Heffley Collection by Scott Heffley – 2007

The Soulful Art of African-American Quilts: Nineteen Bold, Improvisational Projects by Sonie Ruffin – 2007

Alphabet Quilts: Letters for All Ages by Bea Oglesby – 2007

Beyond the Basics: A Potpourri of Quiltmaking Techniques by Kathy Delaney – 2007

Golden's Journal: 20 Sampler Blocks Honoring Prairie Farm Life by Christina DeArmond, Eula Lang and Kaye Spitzli – 2007

Borderland in Butternut and Blue: A Sampler Quilt to Recall the Civil War Along the Kansas/Missouri Border by Barbara Brackman – 2007

Come to the Fair: Quilts that Celebrate State Fair Traditions by Edie McGinnis – 2007

Cotton and Wool: Miss Jump's Farewell by Linda Brannock – 2007

You're Invited! Quilts and Homes to Inspire by Barb Adams and Alma Allen, Blackbird Designs – 2007

Portable Patchwork: Who Says You Can't Take it With You? by Donna Thomas – 2008

Quilts for Rosie: Paper Piecing Patterns from the '40s by Carolyn Cullinan McCormick – 2008

Fruit Salad: Appliqué Designs for Delicious Quilts by Bea Oglesby – 2008

Red, Green and Beyond by Nancy Hornback and Terry Clothier Thompson – 2008

A Dusty Garden Grows by Terry Clothier Thompson – 2008

We Gather Together: A Harvest of Quilts by Jan Patek – 2008

With These Hands: 19th Century-Inspired Primitive Projects for Your Home by Maggie Bonanomi – 2008

As the Cold Wind Blows by Barb Adams and Alma Allen – 2008

Caring for Your Quilts: Textile Conservation, Repair and Storage by Hallye Bone – 2008

The Circuit Rider's Quilt: An Album Quilt Honoring a Beloved Minister by Jenifer Dick – 2008

Embroidered Quilts: From Hands and Hearts by Christina DeArmond, Eula Lang and Kaye Spitzli – 2008

Reminiscing: A Whimsicals Collections by Terri Degenkolb – 2008

Scraps and Shirttails: Reuse, Re-purpose and Recycle! The Art of Green Quilting by Bonnie Hunter – 2008

Flora Botanica: Quilts from the Spencer Museum of Art by Barbara Brackman – 2009

Making Memories: Simple Quilts from Cherished Clothing by Deb Rowden – 2009

Pots de Fleurs: A Garden of Applique Techniques by Kathy Delaney – 2009

Wedding Ring, Pickle Dish and More: Paper Piecing Curves by Carolyn McCormick – 2009

The Graceful Garden: A Jacobean Fantasy Quilt by Denise Sheehan – 2009

My Stars: Patterns from The Kansas City Star, Volume I – 2009

Opening Day: 14 Quilts Celebrating the Life and Times of Negro Leagues Baseball by Sonie Ruffin – 2009

St. Louis Stars: Nine Unique Quilts that Spark by Toby Lischko – 2009

Whimsyland: Be Cre8ive with Lizzie B by Liz & Beth Hawkins – 2009

Cradle to Cradle by Barbara Jones of Quilt Soup – 2009

Pick of the Seasons: Quilts to Inspire You Through the Year by Tammy Johnson and Avis Shirer of Joined at the Hip – 2009

Across the Pond: Projects Inspired by Quilts of the British Isles by Bettina Havig – 2009

Flags of the American Revolution by Jan Patek – 2009

Get Your Stitch on Route 66: Quilts from the Mother Road by Christina DeArmond, Eula Lang and Kaye Spitzli from Of One Mind – 2009

Gone to Texas: Quilts from a Pioneer Woman's Journals by Betsy Chutchian – 2009

My Stars II: Patterns from The Kansas City Star, Volume II – 2009

Nature's Offerings: Primitive Projects Inspired by the Four Seasons by Maggie Bonanomi – 2009

Quilts of the Golden West: Mining the History of the Gold and Silver Rush by Cindy Brick – 2009

Women of Influence: 12 Leaders of the Suffrage Movement by Sarah Maxwell and Dolores Smith – 2009

Project Books:

Fan Quilt Memories by Jeanne Poore – 2000

Santa's Parade of Nursery Rhymes by Jeanne Poore – 2001

As the Crow Flies by Edie McGinnis – 2007

Sweet Inspirations by Pam Manning – 2007

Quilts Through the Camera's Eye by Terry Clothier Thompson – 2007

Louisa May Alcott: Quilts of Her Life, Her Work, Her Heart by Terry Clothier Thompson – 2008

The Lincoln Museum Quilt: A Reproduction for Abe's Frontier Cabin by Barbara Brackman and Deb Rowden – 2008

Dinosaurs - Stomp, Chomp and Roar by Pam Manning – 2008

Carrie Hall's Sampler: Favorite Blocks from a Classic Pattern Collection by Barbara Brackman – 2008

Just Desserts: Quick Quilts Using Pre-cut Fabrics by Edie McGinnis – 2009

Christmas at Home: Quilts for Your Holiday Traditions by Christina DeArmond, Eula Lang and Kaye Spitzli - 2009

Geese in the Rose Garden by Dawn Heese – 2009

Winter Trees by Jane Kennedy – 2009

Ruby Red Dots: Fanciful Circle-Inspired Designs by Sheri M. Howard – 2009

Queen Bees Mysteries:

Murders on Elderberry Road by Sally Goldenbaum – 2003

A Murder of Taste by Sally Goldenbaum – 2004

Murder on a Starry Night by Sally Goldenbaum – 2005

Dog-Gone Murder by Marnette Falley – 2008

DVD Projects:

The Kansas City Stars: A Quilting Legacy – 2008

—30—